A Source Book of Commercial Vehicles

A Source Book of
Commercial Vehicles
Compiled by the Olyslager Organisation
Research by Denis N. Miller
Edited by Bart H. Vanderveen

First published in Great Britain in 1972 by Ward Lock Limited

This edition published in 2008 by Bounty Books,
a division of Octopus Publishing Group Ltd
2–4 Heron Quays, London E14 4JP
www.octopusbooks.co.uk

An Hachette Livre UK Company
www.hachettelivre.co.uk

ISBN: 978-0-753717-82-0

A CIP catalogue record for this book is available from the British Library

Printed and bound in China

All efforts have been made to trace the copyright holders prior to publication, but this has not
always been possible. If notified, the publisher would be pleased to rectify any errors or
omissions at the earliest opportunity.

Foreword

The development of the commercial vehicle is so complex that it would take far more than one volume to explain and record it in any detail. However, there have been certain distinct trends which can be easily followed and these will be found within this 'Source Book'.

Much of this book revolves around the petrol or diesel truck or van, with brief references to battery-electric, producer gas and, occasionally, steam propulsion. All these had a considerable influence on the development of the commercial truck but none more so than the diesel or heavy oil engine. Although more powerful diesels are certain to appear over the next few years, diesel engine design is now claimed to have reached its peak. Designers are searching for new methods of propulsion. The gas-turbine is one. Leading manufacturers such as Ford, General Motors and British Leyland have already developed prototypes and pre-production models, some of which are currently undergoing trials and evaluation under normal operating conditions. The gas-turbine, it is felt, is the answer for long-distance trunking operations where sustained high-speed motor- and freeway running is common. The diesel will undoubtedly come into its own, as, indeed, it has already, as a prime mover for construction vehicles where varying operating conditions are rife and in which vehicle life expectancy is reduced to as little as three years or even priced into a particular contract.

Early commercial truck designs were built along similar lines to passenger models. To increase the capacity of passenger types (buses, coaches, etc.), however, an underfloor-engined layout was adopted, notably in Germany, before World War II and from that time passenger types have rarely kept to the old goods vehicle layout of normal- or forward-control with engine ahead or beneath the cab, major exception being the typical American 'school bus' type. Occasionally, however, the reverse has been true and a few commercials have featured underfloor engines (i.e. Sentinel, Büssing, etc.). Generally, these have sold in relatively small numbers.

Many under-developed countries which, until recently, had no facilities for building commercial vehicles, can now boast extensive assembly plants for such equipment. The larger manufacturers have set up such facilities using local labour and shipping vehicles in CKD (completely knocked down) form. These are assembled on the spot, fitted with locally built bodies and sold throughout the area. Typical examples of this type of operation can be found throughout Africa where many assembly plants now design and build their own cab units also. It is the truck and bus industry which is doing more than anything else to further the development of these 'emergent states'.

Piet Olyslager M S I A, M S A E, K I V I

Introduction

From the dawn of time civilization has engaged in a continual search for improvement. The greatest advances have undoubtedly occurred during the last one hundred years, however, and one single industry has benefited more than any other — transportation. In this context we, in particular, are interested in the commercial road transport industry, the lifeblood not just of the nation but of the world as a whole.

In *A Source Book of Motor-Cars* it was described how the Frenchman, Nicolas Cugnot, an artillery officer in the French Army, designed and built what is believed to have been the first successful mechanically propelled vehicle, in 1769. This, then, requires no further explanation. We shall, instead, advance to the year 1772.

Residing in America at that time was a Welsh inventor, one Oliver Evans who, in 1772, investigated the possibility of applying steam power to the movement of a carriage upon the road. In 1787 he was granted the exclusive right to manufacture and use his improvements for a steam wagon in the state of Maryland and although no actual wagon materialized it is on record that in 1804 he fitted wheels beneath a 20-ton piece of steam dredging machinery and drove it under its own power to the River Schuylkill before sailing to Delaware! This must certainly have been the world's first amphibious craft. It can be seen from this that a need for heavy road haulage was appreciated by engineers even this far back and this basic need is the essence of our story.

Steam vehicles will be dealt with in a later volume in this series. Instead, we will concentrate on the internal-combustion engined road haulage vehicle.

Without a doubt, the 'father' of the internal-combustion engine was Gottlieb Daimler, a German who, from 1872 until 1882, was Technical Director of the Deutz gas engine plant. It was there that he developed his thoughts and designs for a light and compact road vehicle engine.

Daimler's first machine was a motorized bicycle in 1885, followed one year later by a 4-wheeled motor carriage powered by a vertical single-cylinder engine. Simultaneously, Karl Benz had also built a self-propelled vehicle, a 3-wheeled carriage of $\frac{2}{3}$ hp which, on 3 July 1886, attained a most encouraging speed of 9 mph.

The years 1895 and 1896 are well described as the dawn of the internal-combustion engined commercial vehicle in France, Germany, the USA and the United Kingdom. The Germans, as we have seen, were well advanced in the engine field and supplied some of the first units for automotive applications in America. Richard F. Stewart, of Pocantico Hills, New York, for instance, used a 2 hp Daimler engine and internal gear drive for his 1895 wagon, and two years later the first commercial sale in the USA — two electric delivery wagons built by the American Electric Vehicle Company — was made to a Chicago businessman.

In Britain, earlier Government legislation designed to halt progress in the steam vehicle field, continued to hamper operations. Gradually, the United Kingdom was falling behind in the race for improvement. The British Government, therefore, was forced to repeal the crippling 'Red Flag' Act in 1896, opening the door for the full-scale development of road transport in Britain. Although other countries had a good 'head start', British inventors had not been idle during the restricted period and a wealth of experience had been accumulated during those years.

TEA ROSE & WHITE ROSE
AMERICAN LAMP OILS

10

The earliest British trucks, such as this Thornycroft paraffin tanker, bore little resemblance to today's giants. The 'radiator' is of particular interest.

Up to now, commercial vehicle development generally had kept pace with that of the private car. Many of the early models, in fact, were no more than box bodies mounted on motor-car chassis. Despite the fact that British engineers were soon to catch up with their overseas counterparts, it was a foreign commercial wagon, a 4 hp Daimler-engined Panhard-designed van (Daimler engine rights had, by this time, passed to Panhard et Levassor of France), which earned the distinction of being the first petrol-engined commercial vehicle to be sold in Britain, in 1897.

By 1899 the German Daimler concern was exporting 50 per cent of its vehicle production, which included private cars, trucks, vans, taxicabs, municipal vehicles, emergency service machines and many more specialized types. A large percentage of these went to Britain.

Even so, the British truck industry was rapidly gaining ground. Firms such as John I. Thornycroft, the Lancashire Steam Motor Co. (later Leyland Motors Ltd.), and others, were already engaged in the manufacture of steam-powered commercial wagons. Certainly, it would not be long before British-designed internal-combustion engined types made their appearance in large numbers.

Shortly before 1900 some interesting designs materialized in the USA. There was particular enthusiasm for electric traction, principally for light city and urban delivery work, although what are believed to have been the first heavy-duty American trucks, powered by electricity, were built by the Riker Electric Motor Company in 1898 and 1899. Small numbers of compressed-air trucks were also delivered, notably by the International Power Company. These, however, proved impractical.

Great Britain was by far the greatest exponent of the steam vehicle in those early days. So much so that other countries followed British trends in this field. In the USA, this proved to be to the cost of the companies concerned. The American public, being used to the electric-propelled machine for a number of years, did not take kindly to these snorting giants and few were allowed to reach large-scale production. Unlike Great Britain, where steam was to remain in the heavy-duty 'front line' at least until Government legislation and the diesel engine forced it out in the Thirties, American manufacturers concentrated on the petrol-engined machine as a heavy-duty load mover.

By the early 1900s it was realized that not only did the general public need educating in the rudiments and advantages of commercial truck manufacture and use but potential customers did also. Thus, the first Commercial Vehicle Trials were inaugurated. The Liverpool Trials of 1898, 1899 and 1901 for steam-powered machines came first. Other bodies, such as the Automobile Club of America in 1903, organized similar events, based mainly on the French trials of 1897. The two-day American Trials featured steam-, petrol- and electric-powered machines, but many prominent names were missing. The outcome of these American Trials was a resounding success for the internal-combustion engined truck. In 1904 further American trials were held, with the difference that these were conducted under actual operating conditions, each entry being allotted five working days in the service of the American and Wescott Express Companies.

The introduction of the first automotive trade publications at the turn of the century, and the British Government's Motor Car Act of 1903, which increased the general speed limit to 20 mph, also did much to promote the use of mechanical road transport. The first American journal of this type was *The Horseless Age*, introduced in November 1895, with *The Commercial Vehicle*, *Power Wagon and Motor Traffic* following in Great Britain and the United States in 1906. Most famous of all, however, must be *The Commercial Motor*, published by the London-based Temple Press, which made its appearance on 16 March

1905 and, without a doubt, had a very pronounced influence upon the British and, indirectly, the world's commercial truck industry.

Military applications of the self-propelled vehicle have frequently appeared well before civilian production models. As early as 1900 the German Army was experimenting with a Daimler truck, believed to be one of the first commercials to feature a shaft-driven 'live' rear axle with differential, contrasting with the then almost universal chain-drive layout. Before this, of course, the military had frequently used steam-powered machines and continued to do so in fairly small numbers for several years.

By 1904 self-propelled commercials were relatively commonplace. The majority were of 10-cwt to 3-tons capacity, with a few (including practically all steam-powered machines) of higher capacities.

So far as design and layout were concerned, these early types varied considerably. Daimler, for instance, at first favoured the rear-engined belt-driven type with a forward-control layout. In appearance, it was very much like a horse and cart without the horse. Later designs both from Daimler and the French Panhard concern, both of which set the standard for European marques for many years, incorporated a front-mounted engine with driver located behind. This arrangement was, and still is, referred to as normal-control or bonneted. Daimler's rival, Benz, on the other hand, preferred a front-mounted engine located beneath the driver. This is known as the forward-control or 'cab-over-engine' design. It is interesting to note at this point that the 'cab-over-engine' layout, being exceedingly common in the United States, was frequently referred to as the 'American' design. For comfort and safety's sake, however, a number of American manufacturers were soon adopting the standard European normal-control layout.

By 1910 many more new ideas had been tried, adopted or rejected. There were now hundreds of

This 'overtype' design was the first vehicle to carry the GMC emblem, in 1908. The 'cab-over-engine' design was quite normal in the United States at this time.

truck manufacturers throughout the world. Only time could show who would succeed and who would fail. At this time there was considerable enthusiasm in the United States for the 'assembled' truck, comprising component parts purchased from specialist manufacturers. Companies specializing in this type of vehicle claimed that such designs used only the proven units, but stories concerning certain vehicles of this type are certainly inclined to make one think otherwise. Certainly, however, there were successful marques of this type, such as Acme, Federal, etc.

In 1909 the first British War Department 'Subsidy' Trials were held, with the 'Subsidy' scheme itself inaugurated in 1911. Under the scheme, any operator running a vehicle which complied with certain War Department specifications, was paid a subsidy of £120 per vehicle per year, provided it was made available to the War Department in a national emergency.

This scheme was, to put it mildly, brilliant. It was inaugurated at precisely the right time and enabled the War Department to build up a vast fleet of military vehicles within weeks of the declaration of war in 1914. 'Subsidy'-type vehicles, re-conditioned after war service, as well as new models based on 'subsidy' designs, were to take a major place in the development of long-distance road transportation in Britain between the wars. Other nations involved in World War I developed vehicles along similar lines, such as America's 'Liberty' truck, and captured chassis often acted as useful prototypes for further improvements.

1911 marked another important step in the development of the motor vehicle, notably in the United States. Suddenly, there was a trend towards the pooling of resources, both technically and materially. Many small manufacturers began to merge, often with rivals, to form more powerful organizations with increased sales outlets and additional knowledge. Two of these were the Rapid and Reliance types which, from 1911,

Battery-electric vehicles have been generally limited to 1-ton payload capacity apart from a few prototypes such as this early Tilling–Stevens electric. Batteries were stored under the bonnet. Later, Tilling–Stevens were to become famous for their petrol-electric transmission systems.

were manufactured under the GMC banner. Other firms joined with them and still more formed other organizations. The battle for supremacy was on.

Manufacturers, with the large numbers of trade publications and newspapers open to them, were becoming increasingly aware of the value of publicity and promotional activities. Between 1911 and the outbreak of war many took advantage of these facilities and staged trans-continental runs to show off their products. For example, in 1909 a Scania truck, with ball-bearing wheels, created a sensation by travelling from Malmö to Stockholm in thirty-two hours! As a publicity 'bonus' Sven Wingvist, the inventor of the spherical ball bearing, rode along on the trip.

Similarly, but perhaps more spectacularly, a Swiss-designed Saurer, built at the Plainfield, New Jersey, works of the Saurer Motor Company, undertook a journey from Denver, Colorado, to the West Coast. It was carried by rail to Pueblo, Colorado, and arrived without a scratch in New York some five months after the journey had commenced! Other manufacturers were quick to follow these early enterprising examples.

Wheels and tyres were a continual problem. The solid rubber tyre, which had been in use almost universally since the beginning of the century, was not capable of sustained 'high-speed' running which many trucks were by now able to maintain. Surprisingly, perhaps, the pneumatic tyre, developed by the Michelin brothers, had been introduced back in 1895 but still a suitable truck tyre had not been found. With the greater emphasis placed upon commercial road transportation as a means to winning the war effort, the pneumatic truck tyre had appeared at least in the United States by 1917 and by 1919 was optional equipment for most 2-ton and lighter American models. It was to be a number of years before vehicles above this weight had the luxury of pneumatics.

As early as 1898 John I. Thornycroft & Co. Ltd.

The first vehicle off Ford's new Dagenham production line was a Model 'A' van. This was in October 1931.

had built what is believed to have been the world's first articulated self-propelled vehicle, a steamer. This theme was taken one step further in 1912 by a Mr C. H. Martin, of the Martin Carriage Works, York, Pennsylvania, who, in conjunction with the Knox Motors Company, designed and built the 3-wheeled Knox-Martin 'mechanical horse' to motorize any previously horse-drawn wagon. Four-wheel drive also appeared at about this time, introduced in large numbers by the Four Wheel Drive Auto Co., of Clintonville, Wisconsin, in 1912 following experiments since 1909, and shortly afterwards the Jeffery 'Quad', a 4×4 four-wheel braked, four-wheel steer machine, made its appearance.

The end of World War I saw many more developments. An American, Malcolm Loughhead (Lockheed), for instance, patented the 4-wheeled hydraulic braking system and in 1919 both Dunlop and Goodyear announced pneumatic tyres.

The 1920s were even more important in the development of the commercial vehicle. Despite a general recession in the motor industry immediately following World War I, partly attributable to the vast increase in the numbers of ex-Services trucks available to the civilian market, new developments came thick and fast.

Most notable of all was the diesel or heavy oil engine, which completely transformed the trucking industry and led to the rapid replacement of the steam vehicle as a heavy load-carrier. In 1895 Dr Rudolph Diesel had developed a compression-ignition engine which was eventually named after him. Although called a diesel engine, it did not utilize the same methods as the modern diesel. Instead, it employed air-blast injection designed for operating on a fuel of fine coal dust. Robert Bosch, another German inventor, was one of the first to build precision fuel-injection equipment in quantity and at an acceptable price. Although the diesel engine was one of the greatest advances in modern automotive technology, neither these early

types nor the later Swiss Saurer and German MAN models of 1909 and 1912 were successful, mainly due to the inability of their inventors to make the air-blast fuel-injection principle work satisfactorily in small engines.

It was MAN, however, who scored the first important success in this field when the Bavarian Post Office ordered their 4-cylinder unit exhibited at the 1924 Berlin Motor Show. Saurer and Benz also began having considerable success with diesel vehicles, notably in Great Britain, and in 1927 the light 2-litre French Morton engine appeared, being mounted in a lorry in 1929. The year before this, Britain's first oil-engined truck, a 5-ton Mercedes, appeared, and in 1929 the first British-built oil-engined lorry, a Kerr Stuart, equipped with a 60 bhp McLaren-Benz engine, was announced.

Simultaneously, the British Gardner brothers, with the assistance of Sir Harry Ricardo, had by 1928 developed a direct-injection high-speed marine engine which, by the early Thirties, had

Diesel trucks with drawbar trailers first appeared in Germany during the Thirties, intended for relatively high speeds on the new *Autobahn* (motorway) network. This Hanomag was typical of such long-distance outfits.

been adapted for road use and had more or less cornered the British market. Ultimately, Gardner or Gardner-type engines were adopted by many British and some overseas manufacturers, one notable firm being the Dutch Kromhout concern who at first imported Gardner units and later

The 1950s saw attractive styling applied to goods vehicle design, exemplified by this Spanish Barreiros. Similar designs were popular in most Latin-American countries.

In 1960 Thompson Bros. (Bilston) Ltd., were responsible for an interesting experiment in layout and design in the form of the Thompson 'Autotanker'. This was of integral construction, incorporating Leyland running units and a transverse rear-mounted engine. Cab access was via double doors in the front or through a sliding roof hatch.

This is what can result from restrictive axle load rating in certain American states. The biggest truck ever built by Dodge. The 55 ft long rig had thirteen axles and fifty tyres.

built these under licence, fitting them in all manner of vehicle marques, including Dürkopp, Minerva, Indiana, White, etc.

This was the beginning of the end for the steam lorry. Many established British steam vehicle manufacturers turned to diesel truck production,

some successfully, others not so. While names like Atkinson and Foden live on, others like Fowler, Garrett and Yorkshire died rapidly.

Petrol has, of course, remained in vogue for certain applications. For high-performance work, such as in fire appliances, ambulances, etc., it is ideal, and another popular application is in the light van. For heavy-duty long-distance work it is generally uneconomical. In the United States, however, petrol-engined machines were in the majority until fairly recently — plentiful supplies could be found internally and taxes on this fuel were not so harsh as in other countries. These days, the diesel engine has largely taken over supremacy.

The development of the light goods vehicle has been even more complex than that of heavier models. American enthusiasm for the electric-propelled vehicle at the turn of the century was reflected to a somewhat lesser extent on the continent of Europe and was virtually non-existent in the British Isles. As we have seen, the earliest European light models were based on private car chassis. Between 1912 and 1916, however, a cycle-car boom in the British Isles saw a sudden profusion of light vans based on 3-wheeled chassis, revived once again in the 1930s when operating costs, during the 'Slump' period, were of maximum importance.

The years of World War II saw some of the greatest strides ever in the development and use of commercial vehicles. Extremely rugged construction, frequently in conjunction with all-wheel drive, was necessary for military purposes and after the war many thousands of these machines were made available to civilian users. A large number, in fact, remain in regular use even today, notably for site work, vehicle recovery and heavy haulage. Many World War II vehicles are shown in the companion volume *A Source Book of Military Wheeled Vehicles*.

Manufacturers who gained experience in large-scale military production during these years forged ahead after the war. The production of military models continued alongside new civilian ranges and engine developments or improvements, such as the Commer 2-stroke and the Perkins diesel range.

Since 1950 Government legislation has had a greater effect than ever before upon the commercial vehicle manufacturing and operating industries. Throughout the world, vehicle size and weight have been on the increase and the accent upon driver comfort, training and consequent safety has been uppermost in governmental minds.

The latest safety measures introduced by the British Government, for example, have brought in stricter testing and control for vehicles weighing over three tons unladen, plus a completely revised issuing system for vehicle, operating and driving licences. This can only do good to an industry which is all too frequently used as a 'scapegoat'.

1896
Daimler (D)
8 hp 2-ton

In 1896 the first Daimler truck appeared, built along similar lines to the Company's belt-driven private cars. Early versions had rear-mounted engines but later productions had their power unit beneath the driving-seat, thereby allowing an unrestricted load space. These trucks, of which there were four basic types (4, 6, 8 and 10 hp), were designed for speeds of up to 8 mph and had various body styles available.

Engine: 'Phoenix' 2-cyl. in-line, petrol, 8 hp.
Transmission: 4-speed via belts and jockey pulleys.
Chassis: Wooden with angle-iron crossmembers. Carriage type (full-elliptic) leaf springs at front. Coil springs at rear. Belt-drive with pinions engaging internally-toothed gear wheels attached to rear wheels. Four wooden wheels with steel tyres.
Bodywork: Daimler single-dropside wooden body.

1900
Nesselsdorf (ČS)
15 hp 2-ton

The first commercial vehicle produced by Tatra's Kopřivnice factory was a 15 hp truck powered by a rear under-floor engine driving directly on to the rear wheels. It was equipped with 'tiller' steering and could be supplied either as an open wagon or with a wooden or canvas roof and open sides. Carrying capacity was quite high at 2,000 kg.
Engine: Tatra 2-cyl. horizontal, petrol, 15 hp.
Chassis: Angle-iron sidemembers. Carriage-type (full-elliptic) leaf springs at front. Drive to rear wheels via toothed ring on inside of each wheel. Steel-tyred solid wooden spoked wheels all round.
Bodywork: Tatra wooden triple-dropside body with wooden roof canopy.

1901
Benz (D)
4½ hp truck

The Benz range of trucks was in production from 1897 until 1925, when the Company combined with Daimler to produce Mercedes-Benz trucks, buses and private cars. By 1901, production at the Benz plant in Mannheim included various types of truck, from 4½ to 7 hp, some with forward-mounted engines. The example shown had an engine of this type, located beneath the driver's floor.
Engine: Benz single-cyl., petrol, 4½ hp.
Transmission: 3-speed.
Chassis: Wooden sidemembers with bolted angle-iron crossmembers. Light-duty full-elliptic leaf springs at front, semi-elliptic at rear. Chain-drive. Wooden spoked wheels with solid rubber tyres all round.
Bodywork: Benz single-dropside wooden body.

1902
Rapid (USA)
'One-Lunger'

This was one of the first vehicles to be built by Max Grabowsky, of Detroit, Michigan. By 1913 both the Rapid and the Grabowsky, which he had also built (see under 1910), had disappeared and a new generation of vehicles, marketed under the GMC trade name, had been introduced. This 1902 Rapid was generally referred to as the 'One-Lunger' because of its single-cylinder engine.
Engine: Rapid 1-cyl., petrol.
Chassis: Angle-iron sidemembers with suitable cross-bracing. Leaf springs all round. Double chain-drive from engine to countershaft and thence to rear axle. Wooden spoked wheels with solid rubber tyres all round. Right-hand drive.

1903
Vabis (S)
$1\frac{1}{2}$-ton truck

At the first International Motor Show in Stockholm, Sweden, in May 1903, Vagnfabriksaktiebolaget i Södertelge presented its first truck, a $1\frac{1}{2}$-ton capacity Vabis. This Company built a number of follow-up designs and in 1911 combined with Scania Maskinenfabrik AB, also of Södertelge, to form Scania-Vabis AB (now SAAB-Scania).
Engine: Vabis V-2, petrol, 15 hp.
Chassis: Angle-iron side- and crossmembers. Semi-elliptic leaf springs all round. Propeller shaft drive. Spoked wooden wheels with iron treads all round.
Bodywork: Vabis flat body with open cab.

1904
Leyland (GB)
'Pig'

Since 1897 the Lancashire Steam Motor Company had built a number of experimental and production steam vehicles, including tri-cars and lawn-mowers. In 1904 their first petrol-driven vehicle, a 30-cwt payload normal-control machine known as the 'Pig', appeared. The model name, 'Pig', was more a unanimous decision by those who worked on her than an official model designation, presumably because the engine was an extremely difficult starter.

Engine: Leyland 2-cyl. in-line, petrol, 12 hp.
Transmission: 3-speed, using patent Leyland spherical thrust block.
Chassis: Bolted and riveted angle-iron sidemembers. Semi-elliptic leaf springs all round. Worm-driven rear axle. Iron-shod wheels all round.
Bodywork: Leyland wooden flat body with open cab.

28

1907
Dennis (GB)
Motor tractor

In 1907 Dennis Bros. Ltd. received an order from the South African Railways for the supply of a special motor tractor, capable of hauling a gross load of some 9 tons. The machine, which featured a power unit located centrally behind the driver, was, while still only half complete, put through its paces hauling trailers from the local Friary, Holroyd & Healy's Breweries Ltd. It proved to be a most effective machine.

Engine: Dennis 4-cyl. '4-Square', petrol, 50 hp.

Chassis: Bolted cross- and sidemembers. Semi-elliptic leaf springs all round. Early form of propeller shaft drive to 'live' rear axle. Steel spoke wheels with solid rubber tyres all round, duals at rear.

Bodywork: Dennis steel-panelled body with provision for driver and crew member at front under a protective roof canopy.

1910
Grabowsky (USA)
Delivery van

Between 1908 and 1913 the Grabowsky Power Wagon Co., of
Detroit, Michigan, produced a number of truck, bus and light
van models, all petrol-powered. These were amongst the first
American-built commercials to feature engines projecting from
the front of the vehicle 'European style', beginning the trend
away from the 'cab-over-engine' or forward-control layout
known as 'American'.
Engine: 4-cyl., petrol.
Chassis: Riveted sidemembers. Chain-drive. Solid disc wheels
all round.
Bodywork: Grabowsky wooden integral van body with
open-sided cab.

1910
Knox (USA)
R-5

The Knox 'R-5' was offered with wheelbases of 103 in and
125 in, for bodies of 120 in or 144 in length. The front seats
were positioned on either side of the engine compartment and
the left seat could be tilted back to get to the engine. Although
solid tyres were standard for general haulage work, pneumatics
were available for lighter applications such as that shown here.
Maximum speed was claimed to be 30 mph.
Engine: 4-cyl. in-line, petrol, 40 hp.
Transmission: 3-speed in unit with engine.
Chassis: Semi-elliptic leaf springs all round. Prop shaft drive
to bevel gear differential driving countershaft. Thence by roller
chains to rear wheels on solid forged rear axle. Single
pneumatic tyres all round.
Bodywork: 16-man salvage tender and patrol wagon. Body
divided into five stowage compartments.

30

1911
Berliet (F)
CAT

Cab-over-engine or forward-control types were not altogether popular on the continent of Europe although as early as 1911 the French Berliet concern had designed and built one or two machines of this layout. One of these was the Type 'CAT' 3-tonner, one of the largest vehicles produced by Berliet at that particular time. Many Berliets of similar type were used during World War I.

Engine: Berliet 4-cyl. in-line, petrol, 18 hp.

Transmission: 4-speed.

Chassis: Rolled channel-section sidemembers with bolted crossmembers. Semi-elliptic leaf springs all round. Chain-drive from countershaft to rear axle. Cast steel wheels with solid rubber tyres all round, duals at rear.

31

1911
FBW (CH)
5-ton truck

Franz Brozincevic & Co., of Zürich, Switzerland, introduced what was claimed to be the first 5-ton truck in Europe with propeller shaft drive instead of the more orthodox chain-drive. In general style and layout, however, the new model was very similar to its continental contemporaries.

Engine: 4-cyl. in-line, petrol.
Transmission: 3-speed.
Chassis: Bolted construction. Semi-elliptic leaf springs all round.
Rear-axle drive. Wooden wheels all round with solid tyres, duals at rear.
Bodywork: FBW wooden boxvan body with side roller shutter.

1913
Daimler (GB)
3-ton truck

The Daimler Motor Syndicate Ltd. was formed in Britain in 1893 to handle all German Daimler products in this country. By 1896 a factory was opened at Coventry and soon the first commercials were being produced. Early examples, such as that shown, were on identical lines to their passenger vehicles and were extremely reliable in military service during World War I.
Engine: Daimler 4-cyl. in-line, petrol, 30 hp.
Transmission: 4-speed.
Chassis: Rolled channel-section sidemembers with bolted crossmembers. Semi-elliptic leaf springs all round. Propeller shaft drive to overhead-worm rear axle. Cast steel wheels and solid rubber tyres all round, duals at rear.
Bodywork: Wooden flat 'brewer's dray'.

1913
Hillman (GB)
10 hp 'Light Wagon'

The Hillman Motor Car Company, of Pinley, Coventry, built a number of light commercial types up to 1913. This 10-cwt 10 hp machine was typical of the period but was unusual in that power was supplied by a 2-cylinder 'V' engine. A few light commercials were also built by Hillman during the early Thirties but later most of these models were known as Commers.
Engine: Hillman V-2, petrol, 10 hp.
Transmission: 2-speed (3-speed optional).
Chassis: Channel-section sidemembers with tubular crossmembers. Semi-elliptic leaf springs all round. Bevel-gear rear axle. Spoked wheels with pneumatic tyres all round.
Bodywork: Hillman wooden fixed-side body.

1914
Commer (GB)
'Barnet'

The 'Barnet' range of goods and passenger chassis was built by Commercial Cars Ltd., of Luton, who later became the Rootes-owned Commer Cars Ltd. This particular example, a 3-tonner, was still in regular daily use in Hobart, Tasmania, in 1947 when the photograph was taken. The 'Barnet'-type was developed from the early 'YC'-Series Commer incorporating a patented Lindley constant-mesh transmission with steering column change.
Engine: 4-cyl. in-line, petrol, 25 hp.
Transmission: 3-speed constant-mesh.
Chassis: Bolted and riveted construction. Semi-elliptic leaf springs all round. Chain-drive to rear axle. Hollow-spoke cast-iron wheels with solid rubber tyres all round, duals at rear.
Bodywork: Wooden flat body.

1915
MAN–Saurer (D)
4/5-ton truck

Swiss-designed Saurer trucks were manufactured under licence from 1915 to 1924 by Maschinenfabrik Augsburg-Nürnberg AG (known as MAN). In 1924 MAN commenced production of commercial trucks and buses to its own particular design. One of the first trucks to be built under licence was this 4/5-ton truck of standard continental European design.
Engine: 4-cyl. in-line, petrol, 37 hp.
Transmission: 3-speed.
Chassis: Riveted construction. Semi-elliptic leaf spring suspension. Chain-drive to rear axle. Wooden spoked wheels with solid rubber tyres all round, duals at rear.
Bodywork: MAN-Saurer wooden flat body with canvas cab.

1916
Scania–Vabis (S)
3-ton truck

In 1911 two Swedish truck-manu-
facturing concerns, Scania Maskinenfabrik AB and Vagnfabriksaktiebolaget
i Södertelge, combined to form
Scania-Vabis AB. Until then both
had been competitors and both had
been responsible for certain important
innovations in the commercial truck
field. One of these had been the use
of dramatic publicity to advertise a
truck's potential. In 1909, for example, a Scania truck was driven
from Malmö to Stockholm (about
770 km) in thirty-two hours!
Engine: 4-cyl. in-line, petrol, 40 hp.
Transmission: 3-speed.
Chassis: Riveted construction
sidemembers. Semi-elliptic leaf
springs. Chain-drive. Steel spoke
wheels with solid rubber tyres all
round, duals at rear.
Bodywork: Scania-Vabis all-steel
triple-bin side-tipping coal hauler
body with gravitational tipping.

1917
Wisconsin Duplex (USA)
1-ton 4×4

The Wisconsin Duplex Auto Co., of Clintonville, Wisc., was organized in May 1917 (by W. Besserdich, co-founder of FWD) to develop a four-wheel drive truck for the American 'snow-belt' area. Later the Company moved to Oshkosh, Wisc., and soon the prototype 1-ton 4×4 was assembled in Milwaukee, Wisc. To impress investors, the Oshkosh Motor Truck Mfg. Co. (as it became in 1918) ran the new model up and down the Oshkosh Library steps!

Engine: Reo 4-cyl. in-line, petrol, 32 hp.

Transmission: 3-speed.

Chassis: Quarter-elliptic leaf springs at front. Semi-elliptic leaf springs with coil 'helper' springs at rear. Patent automatic positive-locking centre differential in transfer case. Firestone 'non-skid' tyres.

Bodywork: Wisconsin Duplex stakeside body.

1918
Albion (GB)
A.10

The A.10 3/4-tonner was introduced
in 1910 and production continued,
with minor design changes, until
1926. During World War I some 6,000
of these vehicles were supplied to the
Services with many reconditioned
after the war for civilian use. Two
wheelbase lengths, of 157 and 175 in,
were offered and 3- or 4-speed
transmissions were available.
Engine: Albion 4-cyl. in-line,
petrol, 32 hp.
Transmission: 4-speed.
Chassis: Rolled channel-section
sidemembers. Semi-elliptic leaf
springs all round. Chain-drive to rear
wheels. Cast-iron spoked wheels.
Bodywork: Tilt hood van.

1918
Knox (USA)
Articulated 6-wheeler

The Knox Automobile Company, of Springfield, Massachusetts, was the first to produce these types on a steady production basis. The 3-wheeled Knox-Martin tractor of the 1912–21 period, designed by C. H. Martin of the Martin Carriage Works, York, Pennsylvania, was the first true 3-wheeled 'mechanical horse', designed for the motorized hauling of heavy horse-drawn wagons.
Engine: 4-cyl. in-line, petrol.
Transmission: 3- or 4-speed.
Chassis: Bolted construction, hinged behind cab. Semi-elliptic leaf springs all round. Chain-drive. Solid tyres all round, duals at rear.
Bodywork: Kingpin type coupling and Milinaire single-axle log hauler semi-trailer.

1919
Mack (USA)
AC4 'Bulldog'

The Mack 'Bulldog' range had a very long production run; introduced during World War I, it remained in production, with improvements, for twenty years. Both 4- and 6-cylinder versions were offered, with wheelbase lengths varying from 156 to 198 in. The 4-cylinder version was known as the AC4 and the 6-cylinder model as the AC6.
Engine: Mack 4-cyl. in-line, petrol, 75 bhp.
Transmission: 4-speed.
Chassis: Heat-treated steel channel-section sidemembers with channel-section crossmembers. Semi-elliptic leaf springs all round. Chain-drive to rear wheels via semi-floating countershaft in unit with gearbox. Hollow-spoked cast-steel wheels with solid rubber tyres all round, duals at rear.
Bodywork: Heavy-duty semi-trailer coupling.

38

1919
Thornycroft (GB)
'J'-Type

The 'J'-Type was one of Thornycroft's best-selling products. This particular example, which still exists, was delivered to Thomas Wethered & Sons Ltd., brewers, in 1919 and remained in their care until 1946 when part-exchanged for a new Thornycroft. Over the years it has been fitted with pneumatic tyres, electric lighting and cab door windows. Otherwise it is completely original.
Engine: Thornycroft 4-cyl. in-line, petrol, 40 bhp.
Transmission: 4-speed sliding-mesh.
Chassis: Channel-section sidemembers. Semi-elliptic leaf springs all round. Fully-floating overhead-worm rear axle. Dual tyres at rear.
Bodywork: Thornycroft wooden double-dropside 'brewer's dray'.

1919
Walker (USA)
'K'-Type battery electric

The Walker Vehicle Co., Chicago, Illinois, patented a 1-ton battery-electric van in September 1907. This 1919 model was originally delivered to the Chloride Electrical Co. and sold to Harrods Ltd. ten years later. It is now preserved. Biggest problem was the unladen weight of 25 cwt. Weights and radius of operation have always been limiting factors in the development of the battery-electric vehicle and these are still the most important problems to be surmounted.

Engine: 4 hp electric motor built into rear axle.

Chassis: Leaf spring suspension. Pressed-steel disc wheels with solid rubber tyres all round.

Bodywork: Harrods boxvan; open cab with canopy.

1920
Leyland (GB)
'P'-Series 'Overtype'

The 'overtype' Leyland was one of the more unusual results of a trend towards obtaining greater utilization of body space in the years following World War I. Basically, this example was a 'P'-Series normal-control chassis with the cab mounted on top of the engine. Even in 1920 oil and acetylene lighting were still incorporated in many new models!
Engine: Leyland 4-cyl. in-line, petrol, 50 bhp.
Transmission: 4-speed sliding-mesh.
Chassis: Channel-section side-members. Semi-elliptic leaf springs all round. Cast-steel double-reduction rear axle. Solid tyres all round, duals at rear.
Bodywork: Leyland wooden fixed-side tipping body and wooden partially enclosed cab.

1920
Sterling (USA)
2½-ton truck

Lightest of a range of trucks for up to 7-tons capacity produced by the Sterling Motor Truck Company, Milwaukee, Wisconsin, at this time, the 2½-ton model was typical of the period. World War I had, more than anything else, contributed towards the development of reliable and economical vehicles and this Sterling was just one example of the new breed. Chassis/cab shown was photographed in Britain. Sterling was later taken over by the White Motor Corporation.

Engine: 4-cyl. in-line, petrol, 29 bhp.
Transmission: 3-speed.
Chassis: Semi-elliptic leaf springs all round. Fully-floating worm-driven rear axle. Wooden wheels. 36×5 solid tyres at front, 40×5 solid tyres at rear.

1921
International (USA)
'Speed' $\frac{3}{4}$/1-tonner

The 'Speed' was put on the market late in 1921 and by the following year had become extremely popular, both at home and abroad. This was the first truck from International Harvester to have pneumatic tyres as standard and a radiator conventionally placed ahead of the engine. The 'Speed' range, increased to include models of up to 2½-tons capacity, was eventually discontinued in 1930.
Engine: International 4-cyl. in-line, petrol, 20 bhp.
Transmission: 3-speed.
Chassis: Rolled-steel channel-section with dumb-irons at front. Semi-elliptic leaf springs all round. Wooden artillery wheels with single pneumatic tyres.
Bodywork: Wooden single-dropside stakeside body.

1922
FWD (USA)
Model 'B' 3-ton 4×4

The Model 'B' first appeared in 1912 and large quantities were subsequently produced during World War I. Production continued until approximately 1925 and this particular example was fitted with this unusual body in 1922, for the Cookham (Berks) local authority. A lockable third differential in the transfer case was a special feature of the 'B'. A number of these FWDs were produced in Britain under the name 'Quad'.
Engine: Wisconsin 4-cyl. in-line, petrol, 36 bhp.
Transmission: 3-speed with chain-drive single-speed transfer; permanent all-wheel drive.
Chassis: Channel-section sidemembers. Semi-elliptic leaf springs all round (with cross spring at rear). 36×6 pressed-on solid rubber tyres all round.
Bodywork: Merryweather 500-gallon cesspool emptier.

1923
Autocar (USA)
5-ton 'Overtype'

The 'overtype', or forward-control, goods model was firmly entrenched as a 'front line' unit in the United States. The Autocar 5-tonner featured an engine under the driver's seat, easily accessible from either side via specially detachable panels. This layout was similar to many current engine/cab arrangements. The cab was completely open apart from a roof canopy.
Engine: 4-cyl. in-line, petrol.
Transmission: 4-speed.
Chassis: Pressed-steel channel-section sidemembers. Semi-elliptic leaf springs all round, with supplementary coil springs at rear. Double-reduction rear axle. Wooden spoke wheels with solid rubber tyres, duals at rear.
Bodywork: Steel single-dropside tipper with automatic tailboard release.

44

1924
Crossley (GB)
30/40-cwt 'Subsidy'

The 30/40-cwt 'Subsidy'-type Crossley conformed to requirements of the War Office 'Subsidy' scheme. Owners could claim £120, payable at £40 per annum, if the vehicle's condition and mechanical efficiency were up to standard when inspected. The War Office had the right to requisition at any time. Truck shown is undergoing WO trials before being accepted as suitable.
Engine: Crossley 4-cyl. in-line, petrol, 30 bhp.
Transmission: 4-speed.
Chassis: High-tensile channel-section sidemembers with channel-section crossmembers. Semi-elliptic leaf springs. Fully-floating overhead-worm rear axle. Solid or pneumatic tyres offered.
Bodywork: Crossley WD-pattern full-tilt sided body.

1925
Minerva (B)
'Auto Traction'

Minerva Motors SA started production in 1904. In 1925 the Company acquired the rights to Auto-Traction tractor units, on a design by Chenard-Walker, and produced them until 1940. Production of Minerva trucks started again in 1945 for only two years. Since then the company has built the 'Land-Rover' under licence and a military field car of their own design. The vehicle shown was fitted with a diesel engine by Kromhout about 1932. The tyres are not original.
Engine: Kromhout 4LW 4-cyl. in-line, diesel, 68 bhp.
Transmission: 4-speed.
Chassis: Semi-elliptic leaf springs all round. Spiral-bevel rear axle. Dual tyres at rear.
Bodywork: Semi-trailer coupling. Vehicle shown without semi-trailer. Usually supplied as a complete articulated outfit.

1927
DKW (D)
TV300 Tri-van

There have been periods in the development of commercial road transportation when the light economical tri-van has been in vogue. This was particularly so on the continent of Europe at the end of the Twenties and during the early Thirties. Basically the tri-van, as shown, had a motorcycle type engine in the front unit with handlebars or similar. The 3-wheeled van, on the other hand, was steered by a conventional wheel and was generally of a more enclosed design. This DKW was a predecessor of the present East German Barkas light commercials.

Engine: DKW 1-cyl., petrol, air-cooled, 7 bhp.
Chassis: Main backbone swept up to engine position over front wheel. Semi-elliptic leaf springs at rear. Front-wheel chain-drive.
Bodywork: DKW wooden van with roof storage space.

1928
Dennis (GB)
30-cwt

The 30-cwt Dennis was introduced in 1925 and remained in production well into the Thirties. An unusual feature was the solid-tyred spare wheel. It was maintained that the spare wheel was only for emergency use and thus a solid tyre was considered sufficient. This particular example, acquired for £25, from a Romsey, Hants., garage has now been fully restored and is a regular attender at vehicle rallies. She was originally used by John Barker of Kensington for the carriage of fish but the present body is not original.
Engine: Dennis 4-cyl. in-line, petrol, 18 bhp.
Chassis: Rolled-steel channel-section sidemembers. Semi-elliptic leaf springs all round. Propeller shaft drive to rear axle. Single pneumatic tyres all round with solid rubber-tyred spare.
Bodywork: Clement Butler & Cross of Brentford, composite van.

1929
FWD (GB)
R6T

The FWD-England models were built and assembled entirely in Britain. The 'R6T' was a six-wheel drive machine of short-wheelbase, designed as an artillery tractor. It had a powerful engine-driven winch providing a 7-ton pull. In 1929 FWD Motors Ltd. formed an agreement with AEC Ltd. and later models had certain AEC components, including engines. From 1932–36, when production ceased, the 'R6T' tractor was offered as AEC '850'.

Engine: AEC 6-cyl. in-line, petrol, 95 bhp.

Transmission: AEC 4-speed with FWD 2-speed transfer and hub-reduction gearing.

Chassis: Pressed-steel channel-section sidemembers. Semi-elliptic leaf springs at front, interconnected by centrally-pivoted cross-beam. Bogie type rear suspension, incorporating two inverted semi-elliptic leaf springs. Fully-floating spiral-bevel axles all round, with disengageable drive to front axle. 42×10.5 tyres.

Bodywork: WD-pattern full-tilt.

48

1929
Halley (GB)
'YL'-Type

Halley Industrial Motors Ltd., of Yoker, Glasgow, produced both steam- and petrol-engined vehicles, the former from 1901 to 1907 and the latter from 1901 to 1935. The factory was later acquired by Albion Motors. The 'YL'-Type shown here has been preserved by an enthusiast, Brian Sharp, of Tonbridge, Kent, and is typical of late Twenties production.
Engine: 4-cyl. in-line, petrol, 26 bhp.
Chassis: Channel-section sidemembers with dumb-irons at front. Semi-elliptic leaf springs all round. Propeller shaft drive to rear axle. Dual tyres at rear.
Bodywork: Wooden integral laundry van.

49

1929
Scammell (GB)
100-tonner

In 1928 Mr E. C. Marston of Marstons Road Services Ltd. ordered a special 100-ton Transporter from Scammell Lorries Ltd. It was powered by a 4-cylinder Scammell petrol engine that was replaced in 1932 by a Gardner 6LW diesel, necessitating a forward chassis extension. This machine, and another built a year later, are now in the ownership of J. W. Hardwick, Ewell, Surrey, and Rush Green Motors, Hatfield, Herts.

Engine: Gardner 6LW 6-cyl. in-line, diesel, 102 bhp.

Transmission: 4-speed.

Chassis: Heavy-duty riveted box-section chassis frame. Semi-elliptic leaf springs at front. Trailing arm suspension at driving wheels. Short transversely-oscillating axles mounted on rocking beams at rear of carrier frame. Propeller shaft drive to countershaft differential and via four roller chains to rear axle. Solid tyres.

Bodywork: Heavy-duty turntable coupling and 100-ton Scammell dropframe semi-trailer.

1930
Morris (GB)
'Minor' van

As was the case with virtually all light vans of the day, the Morris 'Minor' van was based on the private car of that name. This was a light 5-cwt capacity model with integral body and double rear doors. The 'Minor' found particular popularity with local authorities, public services and retailers requiring a smart compact vehicle for urban delivery work.
Engine: Morris 4-cyl. in-line, petrol.
Transmission: 3-speed.
Chassis: Channel-section sidemembers with suitable crossbracing. Semi-elliptic leaf springs all round. ¾-floating spiral-bevel rear axle. 27 × 4.40 single tyres all round.
Bodywork: Morris standard integral van.

1930
Tatra (ČS)
T24

The 'T24' was a 3-axle version of the 'T23' 4-wheeled model of 1927. The carrying capacity was greatly increased, from the 'T23's' 4,000 kg to the 'T24's' 6,000 kg. Early models were powered by the popular water-cooled Tatra 4-cylinder petrol engine but later a choice between 6-cylinder petrol or diesel units was available. All models featured single wheels all round.
Engine: Tatra 4-cyl. in-line, petrol, 65 bhp.
Transmission: 4-speed with 2-speed auxiliary.
Chassis: Tubular backbone. Independent suspension all round with swing axles. Coil springs at front and semi-elliptic leaf springs at rear. 40×10½ tyres all round with option of 10.50×20.
Bodywork: Tatra wooden single-dropside with full-tilt cover.

1931
Foden (GB)
'R'-Type

Until 1931 Fodens Ltd. concentrated their entire production facilities on the manufacture of steam-powered vehicles. In that year, however, the Company's first diesel-powered machine, an 'R'-Type 6-tonner, was delivered. It is interesting to note that running gear and all other chassis components were developed from those used on the earlier 'Speed Six' steam lorry.
Engine: Gardner 5LW 5-cyl. in-line, diesel, 85 bhp.
Transmission: 8-speed with two gear-change levers.
Chassis: Pressed-steel channel-section. Semi-elliptic leaf springs all round.
Bodywork: Wooden double-dropside.

1931
Fowler (GB)
'Marathon'

John Fowler & Co. (Leeds) Ltd. are more associated with steam vehicles and industrial diesel engines than with diesel-powered road vehicles. In 1931, however, the Company became one of the first to build a complete diesel lorry, including engine. Three models were offered – the 'Marathon' for general haulage work, the 'Warrior' heavy haulage tractor and the 'Crusader' tipper. The 'Marathon' was offered as a 2- or 3-axle outfit. The latter is shown here.
Engine: Fowler 6-cyl. in-line, diesel, 90 bhp.
Transmission: 4-speed with 2-speed auxiliary.
Chassis: Pressed-steel channel-section sidemembers. Semi-elliptic leaf springs all round. Tandem-drive rear bogie. Pressed-steel wheels with 40×8 tyres, duals at rear.
Bodywork: Wooden flat body.

1931
Hillman (GB)
'Wizard' 75

Designed and manufactured as a private car series, examples of the Hillman 'Wizard' were also supplied for commercial use. The 'Wizard', however, was not very successful in either form and before long was withdrawn from production. It is interesting to note that this was despite a lavish publicity promotion campaign when the range was announced.
Engine: 6-cyl. in-line, petrol, 54 bhp.
Transmission: 4-speed.
Chassis: Pressed-steel sidemembers. Semi-elliptic leaf springs all round. Spiral-bevel rear axle. Oversize tyres all round.
Bodywork: Wooden-sided box with drop tailgate.

1932
Minerva (B)
3P.375

Minerva Motors SA, of Antwerp, manufactured an extensive range of commercial and passenger models with production interrupted only during the years of World War II. Typical of early Thirties production was this model, designed to handle payloads of up to 3,750 kg. The unusual thing about this example was the Kromhout diesel engine. This Dutch concern specialized in converting various marques to diesel traction.

Engine: Kromhout 4LW 4-cyl. in-line, diesel, 68 bhp.

Transmission: 4-speed.

Chassis: Pressed-steel channel-section sidemembers with bolted crossmembers. Frame tapered inwards towards front. Propeller shaft drive to rear axle. Semi-elliptic leaf springs all round. Pneumatic rubber tyres, duals at rear.

Bodywork: All-steel side-loading refuse collector with pedestrian controls for steering, brakes, etc., on right-hand side of cab.

1932
Morris-Commercial (GB)
'C'-Series

When introduced, the 'C'-Series Morris-Commercial range was one of the most advanced mass-produced medium-weight petrol-engined goods models available from a British manufacturer and successors to this range, based on similar designs, were still offered in the late Fifties. By the end of the 1930s the 'C'-Series had become known as the 'CV' model and it was in this form that it was most successful.

Engine: 6-cyl. in-line, petrol, 65 bhp.

Transmission: 4-speed.

Chassis: Pressed-steel channel-section sidemembers. Semi-elliptic leaf springs all round. Spiral-bevel rear axle. 4.33FB×20 8-stud fixing steel disc wheels with 32×6 tyres all round, duals at rear.

Bodywork: Wooden flat body.

56

1933
Fiat (I)
634N

The '634N' made its appearance on the Italian truck market in 1933 and production continued virtually unchanged until 1939. It was designed for operation at 14,000 kg GVW, with a payload of 7,640 kg, and provision was also made for hauling a trailer.
Engine: Fiat 355C 6-cyl. in-line, petrol, 80 bhp.
Transmission: 4-speed.
Chassis: Pressed-steel channel-section sidemembers. Semi-elliptic leaf springs all round. 42×9 tyres.
Bodywork: Single-dropside wooden body with underboxes. With rack for tilt on cab roof.

1933
Scania—Vabis (S)
3557

Although the first 3-axle Scania-Vabis was built as far back as 1924, it was not until the late 1920s that this arrangement found widespread acceptance in Europe. At this time, a standard 2-axle machine could cope with some three or four tons. By adding an extra (non-powered) axle this could be increased to six tons. It is interesting to note that some of these open-bodied Scania-Vabis trucks were equipped with special periscope systems to give the driver a clearer rearward view when laden!
Engine: Scania-Vabis 1565 6-cyl. in-line, petrol, 110 bhp.
Transmission: 4-speed.
Chassis: Channel-section sidemembers. Semi-elliptic leaf springs all round. 8.25×20 tyres all round, duals at rear.
Bodywork: Single-dropside wooden body.

1934
Bedford (GB)
'W'-Series 2-tonner

The first Bedford truck, a 2-tonner, appeared in April 1931. Based on the Chevrolet commercial range, which had been assembled in Hendon, North West London, for a number of years, the new model was of normal-control layout available in two wheelbase lengths — of 131 in and 157 in. Before long semi-trailer manufacturers were adapting the 2-tonner for articulated operation, an application for which it was ideally suited.

Engine: Bedford 6-cyl. in-line, petrol, 44 bhp.
Transmission: 4-speed.
Chassis: Pressed-steel channel-section sidemembers. Semi-elliptic leaf springs all round. 'I'-section front axle. Fully-floating spiral-bevel rear axle. 32 × 6.00 tyres all round with duals on driving and semi-trailer axles.
Bodywork: Semi-trailer coupling.

1934
Karrier (GB)
'Cob'

The Karrier 'Cob' 3-wheeler was probably the first true 'mechanical horse' to reach production with a British manufacturer, being introduced in 1931. Developed jointly with the London Midland & Scottish Railway Company, it was designed to take over parcel and distribution services previously done by horses. The example shown is a 1934 4-ton model owned by South African Railways. The 4-tonner was introduced in 1933.

Engine: 4-cyl. in-line, petrol, 27 bhp.
Transmission: 4-speed with chain-drive reduction box.
Chassis: Pressed-steel channel-section sidemembers up-swept at forward end. Semi-elliptic leaf springs at rear. Motorcycle type front suspension. Conventional propeller shaft from reduction box to bevel-gear rear axle.
Bodywork: Automatic ramp-type semi-trailer coupling also suitable for use with converted horse-drawn wagons.

1935
Straussler (H)
15-ton 8-wheeler

The 15-ton Straussler front tandem-drive 8-wheeler was designed by Straussler Mechanization Ltd., of London, and made by Manfred Weiss in Hungary. It was built for the Anglo-Iranian Oil Co. Ltd., who used it on regular runs carrying petrol from the oilfields into Teheran. It was a striking breakaway from conventional practice, with front bogie drive, independent suspension, and ultra-short wheelbase. It was not successful mainly because of steering problems.

Engine: Straussler V-8 petrol, 150 bhp.

Transmission: 6-speed with two gear-change levers.

Chassis: Pressed-steel channel-section sidemembers located back to back with interspersed crossmembers. Independent suspension all round with semi-elliptic leaf springs. CV universally-jointed drive shafts to the four leading wheels. 12.75×20 tyres.

Bodywork: Temporary wooden ballast box. Replaced by 3,700 gallon petroleum spirit tank by Thompson Bros. (Bilston) Ltd.

1935
Thornycroft (GB)
'Beauty' EE/FB4/2

The products of John I. Thornycroft & Co. Ltd. during the 1930s were most impressive. Handbuilt to the last nut and bolt, they included such stirring model names as the 'Amazon', 'Beauty', 'Bulldog', 'Charger', 'Cygnet', 'Dainty', 'Dandy', 'Daring' and 'Stag', to name but a few. The 'Beauty' was a $4\frac{1}{2}$-ton normal-control model offered in two wheelbase lengths. It was typical of the breed and was especially popular with local authorities and brewing concerns.
Engine: Thornycroft FB4/2 4-cyl. in-line, petrol, 55 hp.
Transmission: 4-speed.
Chassis: Pressed-steel channel-section sidemembers. Semi-elliptic leaf springs all round. Fully-floating overhead-worm rear axle. 34×7 tyres.
Bodywork: Single-dropside 3-way wooden tipping body.

1936
Foden (GB)
DG 6-15

The DG 6-15 was the first rigid 8-wheeler from the Foden works and was designed as a short-wheelbase tipper. By 1939 long-wheelbase freight models were also offered, along with 6-wheeled short- and long-wheelbase types and a much expanded 4-wheeled range. After the war a new front grille was introduced for all except the smallest models and the famous 'DG'-Series was discontinued when the Company's 'FG'-Series was introduced.

Engine: Gardner 6LW 6-cyl. in-line, diesel, 102 bhp.

Transmission: 4-speed with 2-speed auxiliary.

Chassis: Semi-elliptic leaf springs all round. Single-drive rear bogie with fully-floating overhead-worm forward axle. 6.00FB×20 wheels. 36×8 tyres, duals at rear.

Bodywork: Double-dropside 3-way wooden tipping body with twin underbody hydraulic rams.

1936
Magirus (D)
M 65

The Berlin International Motor Show, opened by Adolf Hitler in February 1936, proved something of a revelation for outside observers. The accent throughout was on speed, and the use of horizontal engines mounted beneath floor level, with multi-cylinder units particularly popular. The Margirus 'M 65' 6½-ton truck, for instance, featured a horizontal 12-cylinder unit, developed in conjunction with Humboldt-Deutz, slung amidships beneath the chassis and coupled to a Deutz gas producer located behind the cab.

Engine: Magirus 12-cyl. horizontally-opposed, producer gas, 150 bhp.
Transmission: 4-speed.
Chassis: Pressed-steel channel-section sidemembers. Semi-elliptic leaf springs all round. 10.00×20 tyres all round, duals at rear.
Bodywork: Magirus double-dropside composite body.

1937
Commer (GB)
LN5

The 'LN5' goods model was offered as a forward- or normal-control machine powered by a petrol or diesel engine. During the early years of World War II many of the petrol-engined type were converted to run on producer gas. This particular vehicle was one of the first owned by the Cement Marketing Co. Ltd. to be converted in this way, in 1943 – using a Government type gas producer. Unfortunately, this design of producer encroached considerably upon the available load space.
Engine: 6-cyl. in-line, producer gas, 80 bhp.
Transmission: 4-speed.
Chassis: Pressed-steel channel-section sidemembers. Semi-elliptic leaf springs all round. Spiral-bevel rear axle. 32×6 tyres all round, duals at rear.
Bodywork: Shortened wooden flat body.

1937
Praga (ČS)
RN

The Praga 'RN' was a popular goods model throughout Czechoslovakia during the late Thirties. Production of the 'RN' lasted from 1937 until 1944 and during this time a number of variations were built, with slightly altered mechanical specifications, different wheelbase measurements and many other detail changes. Carrying capacity was 2½ tons, maximum speed 80 km/hr.
Engine: 6-cyl. in-line, petrol, 70 bhp.
Transmission: 4-speed.
Chassis: Semi-elliptic leaf springs all round. 7.00×20 tyres, duals at rear.
Bodywork: Single-dropside wooden body with underboxes.

64

1938
Bedford (GB)
WTH 3-tonner

Bedford's normal-control 3-tonner was first introduced in 1934. For 1938 a revised ('bull nose') front-end design was announced, followed by a restyled cab in 1939/40. 1938/39 models utilized the earlier cab style with the new front-end treatment. The example shown here, a 111-in wheelbase tractor unit, was one of these. The later cab incorporated more rounded contours and the bulk of production came after World War II.
Engine: Bedford 6-cyl. in-line, petrol, 72 bhp.
Transmission: 4-speed.
Chassis: Pressed-steel channel-section sidemembers with riveted crossmembers. Semi-elliptic leaf springs all round. Fully-floating rear axle. 32×6 tyres all round, duals at rear.
Bodywork: Scammell automatic coupling and wooden single-axle sided $\frac{3}{4}$-tilt (tilt removed) semi-trailer.

1938
Commer/Unipower (GB)
PM.46 6-wheeled conversion

In February 1938 Commer Cars Ltd.
announced its intention of re-intro-
ducing the 'N5' 5½-tonner, discontinued following the introduction of
the 4/5-ton 'LN5' model in April
1937. Universal Power Drives Ltd.,
of Perivale, Middlesex, who already
marketed a range of specialist forestry
tractors and had undertaken a number
of third axle conversions on earlier
Commer, Bedford and other makes of
goods chassis, designed a similar
conversion for the re-designated 'N5',
necessitating a considerable chassis
extension.
Engine: 6-cyl. in-line, petrol, 85 bhp.
Transmission: 5-speed with
2-speed auxiliary.
Chassis: Pressed-steel channel-
section sidemembers specially
strengthened and lengthened.
Tandem-drive rear bogie with fully-
floating overhead-worm axles.
Bodywork: Double-dropside
wooden body.

1938
GMC (USA/CDN)
2TA

When production of Chevrolet trucks moved to Luton, Bedford-shire, during the early 1930s, the old North London works, at Hendon, Middlesex, were used as an assembly plant for imported North American General Motors products. Certain of these beautifully styled machines, such as the 1½/2-tons capacity van shown here, were extremely popular during the late Thirties, perhaps attributable to their superb power-weight ratio and sheer ruggedness.
Engine: GMC 6-cyl. in-line, petrol, 81 bhp.
Transmission: 3-speed.
Chassis: Semi-elliptic leaf springs all round. Semi-floating spiral-bevel rear axle. 7.50×16 tyres.
Bodywork: Integral van body with double rear doors by Bonallack & Sons Ltd.

1938
Willys-Overland (USA)
1/1½-ton truck

Bulk of production from the Willys-Overland plant consisted of private cars up to 1939 with the famous 'Jeep' appearing during the war years. In 1938, however, a 1/1½-ton truck was introduced and built in small quantities. In common with many other American designs of this period, the Willys-Overland was large and rugged for its weight capacity. It is interesting that the cab doors, windscreen, etc., were the same as those on the private car models. The 2.2-litre L head engine was the same as used in the contemporary Willys car.
Engine: 4-cyl. in-line, petrol, 48 bhp.
Transmission: 4-speed.
Chassis: Pressed-steel channel-section sidemembers. Semi-elliptic leaf springs all round. Fully-floating rear axle. Single tyres.

1939
Citroën (F)
7 TU (Tub 850 kg TA)

Between 1939 and 1940 some 300 of
these machines were produced. For
that time they were a considerable
advance over competitive vehicles in
their class, incorporating as they did
front-wheel drive, a low-loading cargo
area with sliding side loading door,
independent front suspension, and
the maximum use of available load
space. The '7 TU' was, in fact, the
forerunner of the now famous 'HY-
1500' and 'HYP-1600' integral vans.
Engine: 4-cyl. in-line, petrol, 34 bhp.
Transmission: 3-speed.
Chassis: Independent front
suspension with torsion bar
arrangement. Semi-elliptic leaf
springs at rear. 16×45 tyres all round.
Bodywork: Citroën all-steel integral
van body with 2-way loading.

1939
Jensen (GB)
5-ton 6-wheeler

Lorry regulations in the Thirties were prohibitive to say the least. Thus, the Reynolds Tube Co. Ltd., and Jensen Motors Ltd., designed three unique chassisless sided vehicles to carry light-alloy. The first two were made entirely of light-alloy but the third, delivered in 1940, had a steel-panelled wood frame because of war restrictions. This 6-wheeled model had an unladen weight of just under 50 cwt and so escaped some regulations.
Engine: Ford 4-cyl. in-line, petrol, 24 bhp.
Transmission: 5-speed.
Chassis: Integral chassisless construction employing light-alloy throughout. Semi-elliptic leaf springs all round. Drive to forward axle of rear bogie only. Dual tyres at rear.
Bodywork: Jensen light-alloy integral sided body with drop tailboard for 30 ft lengths of steel.

1939
Maudslay (GB)
'Militant'

The 'Militant' was a 168-in wheelbase 6-ton vehicle produced for war use as a military GS (general service) truck. It was originally a civilian model modified to suit military requirements by the addition of a GS body, utility-style cab, WD-pattern towing equipment at the rear, etc. The example shown here was later fitted with a boxvan body for showmen's use and was recently scrapped.
Engine: Gardner 4LW 4-cyl. in-line, diesel, 68 bhp.
Transmission: 4-speed.
Chassis: Pressed-steel channel-section sidemembers. Semi-elliptic leaf springs all round. Fully-floating overhead-worm rear axle. 36×8 tyres all round, duals at rear.
Bodywork: Composite boxvan body.

1940
Hudson (USA)
All-purpose delivery van

The Hudson Motor Car Co., Detroit, Michigan, announced its new all-purpose delivery van in September 1940. Few were actually produced, however, as a number of other prominent manufacturers were turning out similar vehicles at this time. Other Hudson commercial models were based on the Company's well-known car chassis. In 1954 Hudson merged with Nash to become the American Motors Corporation.
Engine: 6-cyl. in-line, petrol.
Transmission: 4-speed.
Chassis: Semi-elliptic leaf springs all round. Rear axle drive.
Bodywork: Special all-steel integral van body with 'easy-access' features essential to multi-stop urban delivery work.

1940
McLaren (GB)
Heavy haulage tractor

J. & H. McLaren Ltd., like John Fowler & Co. (Leeds) Ltd. were essentially steam vehicle builders but they, too, experimented with diesel-powered road vehicles. Only one was built – a specialist heavy haulage tractor of unorthodox layout, employing traction engine type hind wheels, a diesel engine located amidships and a radiator-mounted oil cooler in front.
Engine: McLaren 5-cyl. in-line, diesel, 95 bhp.
Transmission: 4-speed (4 forward and 4 reverse).
Chassis: Semi-elliptic leaf springs at front. Heavy spur gear final drive transmission to rear wheels. 6 ft diameter 'traction engine' type rear wheels with solid rubber tyres. Conventional pneumatics at front.
Bodywork: McLaren composite cab with engine compartment and ballast box behind.

1940
Seddon (GB)
5L

Messrs. Foster & Seddon Ltd., of Salford, Lancashire, commenced production in 1937 with a single prototype, designed by Robert Seddon and weighing less than 50 cwt unladen. The first production models, although limited by the war, became quite popular and were well known for their reliability due to using well-proven and popular proprietary units.
Engine: Perkins P6 6-cyl. in-line, diesel, 65 bhp.
Transmission: 5-speed with overdrive on 5th.
Chassis: Pressed-steel channel-section sidemembers. Semi-elliptic leaf springs all round. Dropped 'I'-section front axle. Fully-floating spiral-bevel rear axle. Pressed-steel disc wheels. 34 × 7 tyres, duals at rear.
Bodywork: Composite flat body.

1941
Guy (GB)
'Vix-Ant'

Coinciding with a partial lifting of the embargo on the sale of new commercial vehicles, Guy Motors Ltd., of Wolverhampton, announced its 3-model 'Vix-Ant' range, available to any British operator holding a Ministry of Transport 'licence to acquire'. These were semi-forward-control machines, one a 150-in. wheelbase rigid truck and the others a 101-in. wheelbase tractor unit and tipper. Cab and bonnet design were similar to the contemporary military 'Ant' trucks.

Engine: 4-cyl. in-line petrol.
Transmission: 4-speed.
Chassis: Pressed-steel channel-section sidemembers. Semi-elliptic leaf springs all round. Spiral-bevel rear axle. 32×6 tyres all round, duals at rear.
Bodywork: Wooden single-dropside tipper with side extensions and single underbody hydraulic ram gear.

1941
Karrier (GB)
KT4

The 'KT4', a four-wheel drive field artillery tractor, was supplied to the India Office (India Store Department) for service with the Indian Army. It was designed for use with 18- and 25-pounder field guns and featured a 5-tons capacity power winch with 120 ft of cable. This machine was generally similar to other British artillery tractors of the period. Karrier, during the war, was also responsible for the production of Humber armoured cars.

Engine: 6-cyl. in-line, petrol, 80 bhp.
Transmission: 4-speed with 2-speed transfer.
Chassis: Semi-elliptic leaf springs all round. 10.50×20 tyres all round.
Bodywork: All-steel welded construction integral body by British Light Steel Pressings Ltd., Acton, London.

1942
Foden (GB)
STG.5

During the war years the Foden 'STG.5' was delivered in large numbers to assist the war effort. It was designed and built as a timber or logging tractor and for this purpose was of an extremely rugged design, having an ultra-short wheelbase, front and rear towing equipment, a rear land anchor and 2-speed 40,000 lb pull winch. Even now, some of these machines are still in regular use, and many have been used as heavy haulage units as well as timber haulers.

Engine: Gardner 5LW 5-cyl. in-line, diesel, 85 bhp.
Transmission: 5-speed.
Chassis: Pressed-steel channel-section sidemembers specially reinforced where necessary.
Overhead-worm rear axle.
Semi-elliptic leaf springs all round.
40×8 tyres all round, duals at rear.
Bodywork: Wooden low-sided with equipment compartments.

1942
Hillman (GB)
10 hp van

From 1942 a variety of light 'commercial' models were produced by Hillman for Services use. These were based on the 92-in wheelbase Hillman 'Minx' car of 1939 and were designed for a variety of uses. The example shown was supplied to the Royal Air Force for servicing airfield lighting. The 3-section roof-mounted ladder could be extended to a maximum of 32 ft. Production ceased in 1943.
Engine: 4-cyl. in-line, petrol, 30 bhp.
Transmission: 4-speed.
Chassis: Semi-elliptic leaf springs all round. Semi-floating rear axle. 5.25×16 tyres all round.
Bodywork: Hillman steel-panelled integral van with double rear doors and roof-mounted angle-iron ladder supports.

1943
Diamond T (USA)
980 Heavy haulage tractor

The '980' was a tandem-drive 6-wheeled (6×4) heavy tractor designed primarily for the recovery and transport of damaged tanks during World War II. A small number of these machines, however, were released to Messrs Pickfords Limited, a leading British heavy haulage contractor, during the war and although basically the same as the military version they were modified for heavy haulage duties. Included in these modifications was the provision of heavy-duty front and rear towing equipment and the original ballast box was modified.
Engine: Hercules DFXE 6-cyl. in-line, diesel, 185 bhp.
Transmission: 4-speed with 3-speed auxiliary.
Chassis: Pressed-steel channel-section reinforced where necessary. Semi-elliptic leaf springs all round. Tandem-drive rear bogie. 12.00×20 tyres all round, duals at rear.
Bodywork: Modified Diamond T all-steel ballast box.

1945
Karrier (GB)
'Bantam' BK tractor

The 'Bantam', in common with other
Karrier models, was most popular
in the municipal field, especially as a
light tipping vehicle for general purposes. It was also successful as a
light tractor unit, and in this form was
more or less a replacement for the
'Cob' 3-wheeled 'mechanical horse'.
The 'Bantam' is still available for certain applications, again mainly for
local authority use, but the current
model bears little similarity to the 1945
version shown here.
Engine: 4-cyl. in-line, petrol, 40 bhp.
Transmission: 4-speed
constant-mesh.
Chassis: Pressed-steel channel-
section sidemembers. Semi-elliptic
leaf springs all round. Bevel-drive
rear axle. 26×6 tyres all round,
duals at rear.
Bodywork: Karrier 'BK'-type
coupling with boxvan semi-trailer
and side roller shutter.

1946
Albion   (GB)
CX27

By introducing their 'CX27' twin-
steering 6-wheeler in June 1938,
Albion Motors Ltd. were able to claim
that they now had a goods model
as standard which not only conformed
to the gross axle loadings of the day
but also to the minimum length
requirements for this type of machine
while capable of carrying a gross load
of 11 tons. Both petrol and diesel
engines were offered and production
of the 'CX27' continued until 1946,
the year in which this particular
example was built.
Engine: Albion 6-cyl. in-line,
diesel, 105 bhp.
Transmission: 4-speed.
Chassis: Pressed-steel channel-
section sidemembers, tapered at rear,
with tubular crossmembers.
Semi-elliptic leaf springs all round.
Overtype-worm rear axle. 36×8 tyres
all round, duals at rear.
Bodywork: Wooden flat platform.

1946
Guy (GB)
'Vixen'

Guy Motors' 'Vixen' 4-tonner was reintroduced in 1946, along with the 'Wolf' 2/3-tonner. Both had been discontinued in favour of military production during the war years and, when reintroduced, were of similar design to their pre-war counterparts. The 'Vixen' was offered in forward- or normal-control form and in a number of wheelbase lengths. The example shown here had a wheelbase of 158 in.
Engine: Guy 4-cyl. in-line, petrol, 58 bhp.
Transmission: 4-speed (constant-mesh on 3rd).
Chassis: Pressed-steel channel-section sidemembers. Semi-elliptic leaf springs all round. Spiral-bevel rear axle. 32×6 tyres, duals at rear.
Bodywork: Wooden double-dropside body.

1946
Morris (GB)
5-cwt van

Of normal-control layout, the Morris 5-cwt of this period was one of the most compact vehicles of its type and certainly one of the most popular, a considerable percentage being employed on Post Office work. Morris vans of the day (there were two models available) effectively filled a gap between the smallest commercial type, the 5-cwt, and the lightest in the Morris-Commercial range, the 'PV'-Series 15/20-cwt model.
Engine: Morris 4-cyl. in-line, petrol, 27 bhp.
Transmission: 3-speed synchromesh.
Chassis: Semi-elliptic leaf springs all round. Spiral-bevel rear axle. Single tyres all round.
Bodywork: Morris standard all-steel integral van.

1946
Scammell (GB)
'Showtrac'

One of the few commercial vehicle manufacturers to design and build a range of internal-combustion engined models specifically for fairground use was Scammell Lorries Ltd. Most famous of these was the 'Showtrac', specially designed and built from 1946 to 1949. Unlike later production, this (the first to leave the factory) featured open bodywork.

Engine: Gardner 6LW 6-cyl. in-line, diesel, 102 bhp.

Transmission: Scammel 6-speed constant-mesh.

Chassis: Pressed-steel channel-section sidemembers, with channel-section front crossmember and all other crossmembers of tubular construction. Semi-elliptic leaf springs all round. Fully-floating spiral-bevel rear axle. 40×8 tyres, duals at rear.

Bodywork: Wooden ballast box body.

1947
Bedford (GB)
'HC' van

Ancestor of the well-known 'HA' van series of the late Sixties and early Seventies, the car-based 'HC'-Series was, in 1947, the smallest vehicle in the Bedford range, having a load capacity of just 672 lb. It was complemented by the 'JC'-Series, a 1,364-lb payload type, with similar mechanical specification to the 'HC'. In 1952, the 'HC' and 'JC' gave way to the highly successful 'CA' range which continued in production, with modifications, until the introduction of the current 'CF' models in 1970.
Engine: Bedford 4-cyl. in-line, petrol, 32 bhp.
Transmission: 3-speed.
Chassis: Independent front suspension with enclosed coil springs. Semi-elliptic leaf springs at rear. Bevel-gear final drive to rear axle.
Bodywork: Bedford integral van.

1947
Nash (USA)
Normal-control truck

Production of Nash trucks commenced in 1917 after Charles Nash, formerly Chairman of General Motors, bought the Thomas B. Jeffery Company, of Kenosha, Wisconsin. Production of the 4×4 Jeffery 'Quad' model was continued with only a change of name. In 1930 production of commercial types ceased, but was revived in 1947 by the Nash-Kelvinator Corporation. When production again ceased, in 1954, some 4,693 trucks of this type had been supplied, only 200 special service trucks being supplied to Nash dealerships on the home market. Cab styling for these models resembled that of contemporary Nash cars.
Engine: 6-cyl. in-line, diesel, 99 bhp.
Transmission: 4-speed.
Chassis: Pressed-steel channel-section sidemembers. Semi-elliptic leaf springs all round. 2-speed rear axle optional. 7.50×20 (8-ply) tyres, duals at rear.

1947
Thornycroft (GB)
'Trusty' PF/NR6

The tandem-drive 'Trusty' 8-wheeler, not to be confused with the normal-control 6-wheeled 'Trusty' of the Fifties, was introduced soon after World War II. This was the first rigid 8-wheeler to leave the Company's Basingstoke works and was claimed as the first production commercial vehicle in the world available with the option of a petrol injection engine. A diesel power unit was standard, with a normal petrol engine as the usual alternative. The petrol injection version was something of a rarity.

Engine: 6-cyl. in-line, diesel, 100 bhp.

Transmission: 4-speed with 2-speed auxiliary.

Chassis: Patented Thornycroft rear suspension system, incorporating four inverted semi-elliptic leaf springs independently pivoted at centres to brackets attached to chassis frame. Fully-floating overhead-worm rear axles.

Bodywork: Double-dropside wooden body specially designed for carriage of bricks.

1948
Austin (GB)
K6

The 'K6' Austin 3-ton 6×4 was employed in various fields
during World War II. Notable examples were RAF signals vans
and REME breakdown gantry vehicles. Many of these machines
entered civilian service after the war, usually with original
bodywork, but a few were completely re-bodied. This example
is just one instance of a re-bodied 'K6'.
Engine: Austin 6-cyl. in-line, petrol, 83 bhp.
Transmission: 4-speed with 2-speed auxiliary.
Chassis: Pressed-steel channel-section sidemembers.
Semi-elliptic leaf springs all round. Tandem-drive rear bogie.
9.00×20 tyres all round.
Bodywork: Bonallack wooden flat body with heavy-duty
wooden bolsters for long lengths of timber.

1948
Morris-Commercial (GB)
'J'-Type

Unlike many vans of the immediate post-war period, the
'J'-Type Morris-Commercial was designed from the start as a
commercial van and had numerous advantages over its competitors. For one, the 'J' had 30 cu. ft. greater carrying capacity
than others in the 10-cwt class and, secondly, it was shorter
than all its competitors which were not of forward-control
layout.
Engine: Morris-Commercial 4-cyl. in-line, petrol, 36 bhp.
Transmission: 3-speed.
Chassis: Pressed-steel channel-section sidemembers with
riveted pressed-steel crossmembers. Semi-elliptic leaf springs
with shock absorbers all round. Semi-floating spiral-bevel rear
axle. 6.00×16 single tyres all round.
Bodywork: Morris-Commercial standard integral all-steel van.

1948
Seddon   (GB)
7L

In its day the Seddon Mk. '7' range was specially popular for local urban delivery work, being small, compact and manoeuvrable, yet still able to gross 12,320 lb in rigid form and 19,040 lb as a tractor unit. The '7L' was the standard 126-in wheelbase goods model, for sided, flat or box bodies, the '7S8' 105-in wheelbase model being designed for tipper work and the '82'-in wheelbase '7S6' for articulated applications.

Engine: Perkins P4 4-cyl. in-line, diesel, 52 bhp.
Transmission: 4-speed constant-mesh.
Chassis: Pressed-steel channel-section with riveted crossmembers. Semi-elliptic leaf springs all round. Girder-section driven rear axle. 4.33×20 wheels with 7.00×20 (10-ply) tyres all round, duals at rear.
Bodywork: Wooden double-dropside body.

1949
AEC (GB)
0854 6×6

After the war vast quantities of ex-Services vehicles came on the civilian market. Many were used in original form whilst others were completely or partially re-bodied. This included the six-wheel drive version of the 'Matador', used as a 2,500-gallon capacity refueller for the Royal Air Force. This was also offered with a petrol engine, identifiable by a fire screen behind the cab.
Engine: AEC 6-cyl. in-line, diesel, 95 bhp.
Transmission: 4-speed with 2-speed transfer.
Chassis: Pressed-steel channel-section sidemembers. Semi-elliptic leaf springs all round, carried at centre of rear bogie by spring chair rotating on fixed centre beam. Double-reduction spiral-bevel front axle. Semi-floating worm-drive rear axles. Split disc wheels with 13.50×20 tyres.
Bodywork: Bonallack fully-enclosed edible oil tank, with steam heating and 2-way flow pump.

1949
Maudslay (GB)
'Meritor'

Now manufacturing commercial truck axles for the British Leyland Motor Corporation, the Maudslay Motor Co. Ltd. were famous for many years as builders of 2-, 3- and 4-axled rigid trucks as well as tractor units. Of these, the 4-axled 'Meritor' was perhaps the best known on the trunk roads of the United Kingdom during the first half of the Fifties.
Engine: 6-cyl. in-line, diesel, 125 bhp.
Transmission: 5-speed.
Chassis: Pressed-steel channel-section sidemembers. Semi-elliptic leaf springs all round. Tandem-drive overhead-worm rear bogie.
Bodywork: Wooden flat body.

1949
Morris-Commercial (GB)
FVO 12/5 5-tonner

Morris-Commercial's forward-control 5-tonner was introduced in April 1948. Power was supplied by a 4½-litre diesel engine manufactured by Morris-Commercial Cars Ltd. under licence from the Swiss Saurer Company, pioneers in the use of diesel engines. The new cab was specially designed to give greater driver comfort, although front-end design was similar to other British marques at this time.
Engine: Morris-Commercial 6-cyl. in-line, diesel, 75 bhp.
Transmission: 4-speed.
Chassis: Pressed-steel channel-section sidemembers with channel-section crossmembers and diagonally-mounted cross-bracings. Semi-elliptic leaf springs all round.
Fully-floating spiral-bevel rear axle. 34×7 tyres all round, duals at rear.
Bodywork: Bonallack integral 'Luton' boxvan with side roller shutter.

1950
Delahaye (F)
'171' 1-ton pick-up

Referred to in sales literature of the day as 'Pickup Large', this sturdily constructed machine was also offered as a 'Pickup Normal', 'Break' (estate car) and ambulance. 1,082 of these were produced from 1949 to 1953 and a special four-wheel drive conversion was offered by Herwaythorn. Some 4×2 pick-ups were used by the French Army in the Trans-African rally early in 1951.
Engine: 6-cyl. in-line, petrol, 100 bhp.
Transmission: 4-speed.
Chassis: Channel section ladder-type frame with X-bracings. Semi-elliptic leaf springs all round. 9.00×16 tyres all round (7.00×16 optional).
Bodywork: Delahaye all-steel pick-up with drop tailboard.

1950
Karrier (GB)
CK3

Karrier Motors' 'CK3' chassis was, at
one time, one of the most successful
British models in local authority use.
It became so popular, in fact, that the
Company was able to offer a standard
range of gully emptiers and refuse
collectors complete ex-works. The
example shown was one of the best
selling from this range.
Engine: 6-cyl. in-line, petrol, 80 bhp.
Transmission: 4-speed.
Chassis: Pressed-steel channel-
section sidemembers. Semi-elliptic
leaf springs all round. Bevel-gear rear
axle. 7.00×20 tyres all round, duals
at rear.
Bodywork: 750-gallon gully emptier
by Yorkshire Engineering.

1950
Pacific (USA)
TR-1, M26/M26A1 6×6

Between 1942—45 the Pacific Car &
Foundry Co., of Renton, Washington,
supplied many heavy six-wheel drive
armoured and 'soft-skin' tractor units
for tank recovery. Many of these were
later employed on civilian heavy
haulage operations, where Robert
Wynn & Sons Ltd. of Newport,
Wales, became renowned for their
six beautifully converted examples —
'Dreadnought', 'Conqueror', 'Enter-
prise', 'Challenger', 'Helpmate' and
'Valiant'. 'Dreadnought' was recently
completely rebuilt, using a number of
Scammell 'Contractor' components,
and re-registered NDW 345G. The
others are now being withdrawn.
Engine: Cummins NHRS6B 6-cyl.
in-line, supercharged diesel, 250 bhp
(de-rated).
Transmission: Self-changing gears
RV30.
Chassis: Pressed-steel channel-
section sidemembers. Chain-drive
to rear bogie. Propeller shaft drive to
front axle.
Bodywork: Wynns coachbuilt
crew-cab and ballast box.

1950
Panhard/Thornton (F)
6-wheeled conversion

The French Panhard et Levassor concern were pioneers in the development of the internal-combustion engined motor vehicle. The firm has concentrated in the main upon private car production. Trucks were made in relatively small quantities. Shown is a 6×4 conversion (by Thornton) of a typical medium-weight chassis. Most post-war Panhard commercials, however, were vans and light trucks, based on the Dyna-Panhard car chassis and its successors.
Engine: Panhard 4-cyl. in-line, diesel, 110 bhp.
Transmission: 5-speed with 2-speed auxiliary.
Chassis: Pressed-steel channel-section sidemembers. Semi-elliptic leaf springs all round. Thornton tandem-drive rear bogie. C.20 tyres all round, duals at rear.
Bodywork: All-steel fixed-side tipper with single underbody hydraulic ram gear.

1951
Austin (GB)
'Loadstar'

Austin's 'Loadstar' range was announced in December 1949 and introduced a new kind of comfort in the British truck industry; including increased leg-room, 3-man seating, sturdy construction and car frontal styling. The 'Loadstar' was available as a 2- or 5-ton long-wheelbase model or as a 5-ton short-wheelbase tipper. The latter was also supplied as a tractor unit as shown.
Engine: Austin 6-cyl. in-line, petrol, 68 bhp.
Transmission: 4-speed.
Chassis: Pressed-steel channel-section sidemembers reinforced by flitch plates where necessary. Semi-elliptic leaf springs all round. Bevel-gear rear axle. 34×7 tyres all round, duals at rear.
Bodywork: Scammell automatic coupling with Scammell single-axle streamlined boxvan semi-trailer.

1951
Vulcan (GB)
6 PF

The Vulcan Motor & Engineering Company commenced commercial vehicle production at Southport, Lancashire, in 1904, and later moved to the Tilling—Stevens plant at Maidstone, Kent. After the war, until the Company joined the Rootes Group in 1953, Vulcan Motors Ltd. became well known as builders of 2-axled rigid and articulated machines of forward-control layout. The '6 PF' was typical of these.

Engine: 6-cyl. in-line, diesel, 70 bhp.
Transmission: 4-speed (with constant-mesh on 3rd).
Chassis: Semi-elliptic leaf springs all round. Overhead-worm rear axle. 8.25 × 20 tyres all round, duals at rear.
Bodywork: Wooden single-dropside tipping body with Telehoist single underbody hydraulic ram.

1952
ACLO (GB)
'Mammoth Major III'

For many years the products of AEC's Southall Works were sold in Latin American countries under the ACLO brand name. These included thirty specially adapted versions of the 'Mammoth Major III' rigid 8-wheeled truck with bodywork by Bonallack & Sons Ltd. These were exported to Brazil in 1952 and an almost identical model, with AEC brand name, was exhibited on the Bonallack Stand at the Commercial Motor Show, Earls Court, London, that year.

Engine: AEC 6-cyl. in-line, diesel, 125 bhp.

Transmission: 5-speed.

Chassis: Pressed-steel channel-section sidemembers. Semi-elliptic leaf springs all round. Single-drive rear bogie with double-reduction forward axle. 10.00×20 (12-ply) tyres all round, duals at rear.

Bodywork: Triple-dropside light-alloy body by Bonallack & Sons Ltd. Cab also by Bonallack, with removable upper half for easy shipment.

1952
Bedford (GB)
OLA 4-tonner

Bedford's 'O'-Series goods and passenger models were amongst the most successful that Vauxhall Motors have ever produced, the 'OB' passenger model being one of the most famous of its day in the United Kingdom. The 'O'-Series has been applied to virtually every type of use, one special example being this mobile shop with wheelbase extension.
Engine: Bedford 6-cyl. in-line, petrol, 84 bhp.
Transmission: 4-speed.
Chassis: Pressed-steel channel-section sidemembers with Baico wheelbase extension. Semi-elliptic leaf springs all round. Hypoid-bevel rear axle. 7.00×20 tyres all round, duals at rear.
Bodywork: Spurlings dual entrance/exit 'Luton' integral mobile shop.

1953
Citroën (F)
'23'-Series

Citroën's '23'-Series was offered as a chassis/cab, integral van or full-tilt dropside truck, with one or two other variations. It was developed from the Company's pre-war normal-control commercial ranges and was designed for operation at 4,500 kg GVW. The integral van featured here was of robust design with large streamlined front wings typical of the period.
Engine: Citroën 4-cyl. in-line, petrol, 50 bhp.
Transmission: 4-speed (with synchromesh on 3rd and 4th).
Chassis: Channel-section sidemembers. Semi-elliptic leaf springs all round. Spiral-bevel rear axle. 6.50×20 tyres all round, duals at rear.
Bodywork: Integral van body ('Fourgon 2 Tonnes').

1953
Standard (GB)
12-cwt van

The 12-cwt van was based on the famous 'Vanguard' saloon, with the same frontal styling, substantial chromium bumper and sturdy construction. Also available was an estate car version and a pick-up, but these were less common. All three were used extensively by the Royal Air Force. The 'Vanguard' was introduced in 1948 and was Standard's first real post-war model.

Engine: 4-cyl. in-line, petrol, 68 bhp.
Transmission: 3-speed.
Chassis: Pressed-steel channel-sections welded together to form rectangular box-section sidemembers, braced by a cruciform member. Independent coil spring suspension at front. Semi-elliptic leaf springs at rear. Controlled by hydraulic dampers, with anti-roll bar at rear. Hypoid bevel-gear rear axle. 6.00×16 tyres all round.
Bodywork: Standard all-steel integral van body with 2.4 cu.m loadspace.

1953
Thornycroft (GB)
'Mighty Antar'

Production of the 'Mighty Antar', one of the largest road tractors ever produced in England, resulted from an enquiry, via George Wimpey & Co. Ltd., from the Iraq Petroleum Company. The first batch was shipped to the Middle East for Iraq Petroleum in 1953. This one, however, was one of two machines supplied for the Snowy Mountains Hydro-Electric Scheme in Australia.

Engine: Rover 'Meteorite' Mk 101 V-8 diesel, 250 bhp.

Transmission: 4-speed constant-mesh with 3-speed auxiliary.

Chassis: Heat-treated alloy-steel channel-section sidemembers with bolted crossmembers. Semi-elliptic leaf springs. Rectangular-section front axle. Tandem-drive rear bogie with double-reduction at each axle. 14.00×24 (20-ply) tyres, duals at rear.

Bodywork: Later equipped with wooden ballast box as independent drawbar tractor.

1954
Douglas (GB)
'Transporter' 4×4

F. L. Douglas (Equipment) Ltd. are manufacturers of specialist automotive machinery. One model was the four-wheel drive 'Transporter', a special short-wheelbase tractor for timber extraction. Using AEC 'Matador' running units, it was like the 'Matador' except for the shorter wheelbase and Mk III AEC cab.

Engine: AEC 6-cyl. in-line, diesel, 125 bhp.
Transmission: 4-speed with 2-speed transfer.
Chassis: Pressed-steel channel-section sidemembers with bolted crossmembers. Semi-elliptic leaf springs. Direct drive from gearbox to fully-floating double-reduction bevel and helical gearing rear axle. Disengageable drive to similar steering front axle.
Bodywork: Wooden flat body with collapsible rear jib crane and land anchor.

1954
Foden (GB)
FE 4/8

By locating the supercharged Foden 2-stroke engine between the driver and passenger, with a second seat mounted over the engine, the 'FE 4/8' 8-tonner provided 'straight-through' access for a crew of three, making it popular with breweries who needed 3-men crews. The engine (8¼ cwt), provided an exceptional performance and, when introduced at Earls Court in 1952, the design was very advanced.

Engine: Foden FD.4 4-cyl. in-line, diesel, 84 bhp.
Transmission: 8-speed.
Chassis: Pressed-steel channel-section sidemembers with bolted pressed-steel crossmembers. Semi-elliptic leaf springs. Fully-floating hypoid rear axle. 9.00×20 (12-ply) tyres, duals at rear.
Bodywork: Single-dropside tipper with twin underbody hydraulic rams.

1954
Leyland (GB)
'Steer'

The Leyland 'Steer' was one of the twin-steer 'Chinese Six' models offered by British manufacturers from 1930–50. The 'Steer' came only as a 228-in wheelbase machine designed for road haulage and large numbers were sold overseas. The 'Hippo' 6-wheeled and 'Octopus' 8-wheeled rigid models were other variants.
Engine: Leyland 6-cyl. in-line, diesel, 125 bhp.
Transmission: 5-speed constant-mesh.
Chassis: Pressed-steel channel-section sidemembers with riveted and bolted crossmembers. Semi-elliptic leaf springs. 'I'-section alloy-steel front axles. Fully-floating overhead-worm rear axle. 3-piece 10-stud steel disc wheels with 36×8 tyres, duals at rear.
Bodywork: Rhodesian-built all-steel triple-dropside.

1955
Austin (GB)
5-ton forward-control

The Austin Motor Co. Ltd. announced its new 5-ton forward-control range in March 1955. This was often referred to as the Series III and was produced simultaneously with the normal-control 'WE'-Series, a follow-up to the earlier 'Loadstar' range. The new model was offered in various wheelbase lengths for use as a rigid goods, tipper or tractor unit. This example is the 160-in wheelbase goods model.
Engine: Austin 6-cyl. in-line, petrol, 87 bhp.
Transmission: 4-speed.
Chassis: Pressed-steel channel-section sidemembers. Semi-elliptic leaf springs all round. Spiral-bevel rear axle. 7.50×20 tyres all round, duals at rear.
Bodywork: Light-alloy double-dropside.

1955
Peugeot (F)
D4A

In October 1955 the Peugeot 'D4' Series of light commercials was introduced. These were developed from the earlier 'D3' Series, which first saw the light of day late in 1941. By the time 'D4' production ceased in May 1965 the 'D4A' had been succeeded by the 'D4AD', 'D4B' and, finally, the 'D4BD', each with detail improvements over their predecessors. The Series could be supplied as a van, personnel carrier or ambulance.
Engine: Peugeot 4-cyl. in-line, petrol, 45 bhp.
Transmission: 4-speed.
Chassis: Independent torsion bar suspension with telescopic hydraulic shock absorbers all round. Front-wheel drive. 19×400 tyres all round.
Bodywork: Peugeot all-steel integral van body of 6.8 cu.m. capacity.

1956
Fiat (I)
615N

This model was designed for use as a compact easily manoeuvrable light delivery truck. The 305B 4-cylinder engine took up the minimum of space ahead of the driver, resulting in a 'snub nose' effect. With two persons in the cab, carrying capacity of the '615N' was 1,500 kg. The '615N' was introduced in 1956 followed by a four-year production run. There was a clear family resemblance between this and the Company's '500' and '600' private car designs.

Engine: Fiat 305B 4-cyl. in-line, diesel, 43 bhp.
Transmission: 4-speed.
Chassis: Pressed-steel channel-section sidemembers. Semi-elliptic leaf springs all round. Conventional rear axle drive. $4\frac{1}{2}$K×16 wheels with 6.00 or 6.40×16 tyres all round, duals at rear.
Bodywork: Fiat single-dropside.

1956
Ford Thames (GB)
4D 4-tonner

Ford's normal-control '4D' and '6D' trucks were originally announced as V-8 petrol-engined vehicles, and were eventually superseded by the famous Thames 'Trader' range. The '4D'-Series was available from 30-cwt to 4-tons payload capacity, the example shown being a 4-ton model.
Engine: Ford 4D 4-cyl. in-line, diesel, 64 bhp.
Transmission: 4-speed.
Chassis: Pressed-steel channel-section sidemembers. Semi-elliptic leaf springs all round. Hypoid-bevel rear axle. 7.50×20 (12-ply) tyres all round, duals at rear.
Bodywork: Flat 'brewer's dray'.

1956
Kromhout (NL)
V5S

Kromhout Motoren Fabriek NV were famous from 1923 onwards for their marine engines but when they discovered that they were being fitted to commercial trucks they decided to produce commercial vehicles for this clientele. The 'V5S' was one of four models, with 4-, 5- or 6-cylinder engines, built under licence from the British Gardner concern, each chassis having a choice of four wheelbase lengths.
Engine: 5G108 5-cyl. in-line, diesel, 100 bhp.
Transmission: 6-speed.
Chassis: Pressed-steel channel-section sidemembers. Semi-elliptic leaf springs. 10.00×20 (16-ply) tyres at front, 9.00×20 (14-ply) dual tyres at rear.
Bodywork: Double-dropside composite body by Deckers en Zonen, Leiden.

1957
AEC (GB)
'Mercury'

One of the most popular British 2-axle medium-weight goods models of the Fifties and Sixties was the 'Mercury' 12/14-tons gross range. Many leading haulage and oil companies standardized on the 'Mercury' at the lighter end of their fleets, particularly when heavier AEC models were also operated as there was some interchangeability of components. These early 'Mercury' trucks are now largely superseded by the 'Ergomatic'-cabbed ranges.

Engine: AEC AV470 6-cyl. in-line, diesel, 112 bhp.
Transmission: 5-speed synchromesh.
Chassis: Pressed-steel channel-section sidemembers with pressed-steel channel-section crossmembers. Semi-elliptic leaf springs. Fully-floating single-reduction spiral-bevel rear axle. B7.0 steel disc wheels with 10.00 × 20 (14-ply) tyres, duals at rear.
Bodywork: Bonallack 4-compartment elliptical petroleum spirit tank body.

100

1957
Berliet (F)
T100

The huge 'T100' still lays claim to being the largest commercial truck in the world. Designed principally for desert use, it was available as a six-wheel drive cargo or dump truck or as a six-wheel drive tractor, at 201,600 lb GVW or 280,000 lb GCW respectively. A 700 bhp engine was optional.

Engine: Cummins V-12, diesel, 600 bhp.
Transmission: 4-speed with 2-speed transfer.
Chassis: 37.5×33 tyres all round, single at rear.
Bodywork: All-steel oilfields-type flat with stakesides, headache rack and winch gear.

1957
Bernard (F)
4R.150

Camions Bernard, of Arcueil, Seine, France, concentrated upon
normal-control goods models although, a few years ago, one
or two forward-control designs were also produced. Normal-
control models were built to the same basic design from the
1950s. A special feature was the low-loading qualities of many
models, effected by extremely deep and low-slung chassis
frame sidemembers.
Engine: Bernard 6-cyl. in-line, diesel, 120 bhp.
Transmission: 5-speed (or optional 10-speed).
Chassis: Deep-section pressed-steel channel-section
sidemembers. Semi-elliptic leaf springs with hydraulic shock
absorbers at front. Double-reduction rear axle. F.20 tyres, duals
at rear.
Bodywork: All-steel double-dropside tipper with twin
underbody hydraulic ram gear.

1957
Tempo (D)
'Wiking Rapid'

The Tempo light commercial vehicle range was designed and
built by Vidal und Sohn GmbH, later known as Tempowerk, of
Hamburg. In 1958 it was announced that Jensen Motors Ltd.,
of West Bromwich, Staffordshire, would assemble these
vehicles under licence but although a few prototypes appeared
in the UK quantity production never materialized. All models,
both German- and British-built, featured BMC engines.
Engine: Austin 4-cyl. in-line, petrol, 32 bhp.
Transmission: 4-speed.
Chassis: Tubular sidemembers with channel-section outriggers
for supporting the bodywork. Single transverse leaf spring at
front. Independent rear suspension with coil springs and radius
rods. Driven front wheels via constant-velocity joints. 6.50×16
tyres.
Bodywork: Tempo drop-tailboard pick-up type.

102

1958
De Soto　(GB)
'Kew'

During the 1930s the American Chrysler Corporation introduced badge engineering to expand export sales. This was accomplished by selling Dodge trucks, re-named Fargo or De Soto, through sales outlets other than Dodge. Mechanically, all were identical. Later, this system was adopted by Dodge Bros. (Britain) Ltd. The most popular model to receive this treatment was the 'Kew' normal-control series, from the now defunct Kew (Surrey) plant. This particular example operates in Finland.

Engine: Perkins 6-cyl. in-line, diesel, 104 bhp.

Transmission: 5-speed.

Chassis: Flanged sidemembers. Semi-elliptic leaf springs. Single-speed spiral-bevel rear axle. B6.5×20 3-piece wheels. 9.00×20 (12-ply) tyres, duals at rear.

Bodywork: Locally-built demountable flat body for sawn timber. Equipped with tipping gear and winches to haul body back on to chassis.

103

1958
Guy (GB)
'Invincible' Mk I

When Guy Motors announced its new 'Invincible' 4-, 6- and 8-wheeled forward- and normal-control range for home and overseas in August 1958, the overall design was claimed to be amongst the most advanced available in Europe. This was the first British commercial to incorporate dual headlamps, and it featured a cigarette lighter and electric shaver socket in the list of standard cab refinements. This Mk I version could always be distinguished from the Mk II by its different front bumper arrangement.

Engine: Gardner 6LW 6-cyl. in-line, diesel, 112 bhp.
Transmission: Meadows 450 5-speed.
Chassis: Pressed-steel channel-section sidemembers. Semi-elliptic leaf springs all round. Spiral-bevel rear axle. Heavy-duty B/7 wheels. 10.00×20 tyres, duals at rear.
Bodywork: Double-dropside light-alloy tipping body by Bonallack & Sons Ltd.

1958
Scania–Vabis (S)
L75

The introduction of the normal-control
'L75' series in 1958 brought a string
of new features to the Scania-Vabis
range, including a synchronized
auxiliary transmission, double-reduction rear axle and pneumatically
actuated differential lock. This range
also featured the newly designed D10
engine, which was also produced in
supercharged form developing 205
bhp. In 1969 the Company merged
with Saab, the well-known aircraft
and car manufacturers, and the trucks
were re-named Scania.
Engine: Scania-Vabis D10 6-cyl.
in-line, diesel, 165 bhp.
Transmission: 5-speed
synchromesh.
Chassis: Pressed-steel sidemembers.
Semi-elliptic leaf springs all round.
Single-reduction rear axle.
Bodywork: Wooden fixed-side
full-tilt body.

1958
Simca (F)
90K 'Messagère'

This light all-steel integral van was based on the famous 'Aronde' 1300 private car design and was in production from 1953 until 1962 with occasional styling changes. This, and a similar model known as the 'Commerciale', could carry some 500 kg payload, load access being via dropped and raised tailgates at the rear.
Engine: Simca 'Flash' 1300 4-cyl. in-line, petrol, 45 bhp.
Transmission: 4-speed synchromesh.
Chassis: Independent front suspension with coil springs. Semi-elliptic leaf springs at rear. Shock absorbers all round and stabilizer at front. Hypoid type rear axle. 5.75×15 tyres all round.
Bodywork: Simca all-steel integral van.

1959
Borgward (D)
B 4500

The Carl F. W. Borgward Motoren Werke at Bremen was famous for its private car models until production ceased in 1961. A range of light and medium goods models was also offered, however, ranging from the 1500-Series forward- and normal-control models to the 4500-Series forward-control type.
Engine: 6-cyl. in-line, diesel, 110 bhp.
Transmission: 5-speed.
Chassis: Pressed-steel channel-section sidemembers. Semi-elliptic leaf springs all round with hydraulic shock absorbers at front. 8.25×20 tyres all round, duals at rear.
Bodywork: 5th wheel coupling and Bunge single-axle double-dropside semi-trailer.

1959
Scammell (GB)
8×6 Motorway gritter

When the M1 opened in 1959, the Ministry of Transport met the problem of keeping the new highway open during bad weather. A fleet of high-speed motorway gritters, for operation at 20 and 24 tons GVW, and of 6×6 and 8×6 configuration, was developed. Scammell Lorries Ltd. built a number in the 24 tons 8×6 class, with a unique drive system to both rear axles and the foremost steering axle.

Engine: Leyland 0.680 6-cyl. in-line, diesel, 160 bhp.
Transmission: Scammell 6-speed with 2-speed transfer.
Chassis: Pressed-steel channel-section sidemembers with forward ends reinforced for snowplough attachment. Walking-beam type rear suspension. Double-reduction front driving axle. Overhead-worm axles at rear bogie. 'Trakgrip' tyres, 12.00×20 front, 14.00×20 rear.
Bodywork: Hopper body by Atkinsons' Agricultural Appliances Ltd., Clitheroe, Lancashire. Underfloor grit spinners with hyd. motors powered by separate engine-driven pumps. Straight or 'V'-shaped snowplough blades supplied.

1960
Dennis (GB)
'Teal'

The 'Teal' was introduced in 1956 as an addition to the 'Pax II' range. Principally, it was for use as a pantechnicon for long-distance applications, but it was largely unsuccessful in that certain 'Pax II' models were more economically viable than the 'Teal', being of lighter construction but capable of carrying heavier loads.
Engine: Perkins P6 6-cyl. in-line, diesel, 83 bhp.
Transmission: 5-speed.
Chassis: Semi-elliptic leaf springs all round. Spiral-bevel rear axle.
7.50×20 (10-ply) tyres all round, duals at rear.
Bodywork: Light-alloy integral 'Luton' pantechnicon body by Bonallack & Sons Ltd. Specially designed for carriage of furniture.

1960
Thornycroft (GB)
'Mastiff' MH/QR6

The single-drive 'Mastiff' 6-wheeler was claimed to be way ahead of its time. Its design and construction took sustained motorway runs into account, work for which it was ideally suited both economically and in comfort and handling. It was developed from the 4-wheeled 'Mastiff' but the new model was not merely a 4-wheeler with trailing axle conversion. It was designed throughout as a 6-wheeled truck.
Engine: Thornycroft QR6 6-cyl. in-line, diesel, 130 bhp.
Transmission: 5-speed constant-mesh.
Chassis: Pressed-steel channel-section sidemembers with bolted crossmembers. Semi-elliptic leaf springs. 'I'-section front axle. Single trailing axle. 9.00 × 20 (12-ply) tyres, duals at rear.
Bodywork: Thornycroft flat body.

1960
Trojan (GB)
25-cwt

This 25-cwt forward-control model was announced in 1958 and was first exhibited at the International Commercial Motor Show that year. It was designed as a 13-seat passenger model or integral van but later long- and short-wheelbase types were offered with dropside bodies or in chassis/scuttle or chassis/cab form. This example was the standard long-wheelbase dropside model.
Engine: Perkins P3 3-cyl. in-line, diesel, 41 bhp.
Transmission: 4-speed.
Chassis: Straight sidemembers of box-section. Independent trailing arm front suspension with semi-elliptic leaf springs at rear. $\frac{3}{4}$-floating hypoid-drive rear axle. Steel disc wheels with 6.50 × 16 (8-ply) tyres.
Bodywork: Trojan single-dropside wooden body.

GAZEWAY PLANT HIRE LTD

1961
Bristol (GB)
HA6LL Series 185

Since road haulage nationalization in 1947, Bristol Commercial Vehicles Ltd. have produced a number of interesting articulated and rigid 8-wheeled models for British Road Services Ltd. only. This was because the Bristol organization was part of the British Transport Commission and was only permitted to supply BTC member companies, of which BRS was one. The 'HA6LL' was a 4-wheeled unit with a colour-impregnated one-piece glassfibre cab moulding and claimed to be the best in the BRS fleet.

Engine: Leyland 0.680 6-cyl. in-line, diesel, 150 bhp.

Transmission: 5-speed constant-mesh.

Chassis: Pressed-steel channel-section sidemembers. Semi-elliptic leaf springs. Spiral-bevel rear axle. 9.00×20 (12-ply) tyres, duals at rear.

Bodywork: 5th wheel coupling. Normally supplied complete with tandem-axle flat semi-trailer.

1961
Fiat (I)
690T

In Italy in the early 1960s, operators and manufacturers were striving to solve the problems associated with increased gross vehicle weights and load distribution. One answer was to fit a second steering axle and qualify the converted vehicle for a higher gross load rating. Manufacturers such as Fiat engaged specialist conversion firms like Viberti to supply this equipment direct to the factory, to produce twin-steer 6-wheeled trucks and tractors ex works. The '690T' was one of these.

Engine: Fiat 203 6-cyl. in-line, diesel, 152 bhp.
Transmission: 8-speed.
Chassis: Pressed-steel channel-section sidemembers with rear of chassis frame tapered downwards to facilitate coupling and uncoupling of semi-trailer. Rear axle drive. 11.00×20 (14-ply) tyres, duals at rear.
Bodywork: 5th wheel coupling.

1961
Goggomobil (D)
TL 400 Pick-up

Hans Glas GmbH introduced its
light pick-up as a logical addition to
its 300 and 400 van range. All models
were of the same basic design,
employing a 15 or 20 bhp engine
located at the rear, an electro-magnetic pre-selective transmission,
four-wheel hydraulic brakes and
swing axles. The example shown had
a 6-cwt load capacity.
Engine: Glas 03 2-cyl. in-line,
petrol, 20 bhp.
Transmission: 4-speed with
electro-magnetic pre-selection.
Chassis: Swing axles with helical
springs and hydraulic shock absorbers
all round. 4.80×10 tyres all round.
Bodywork: All-steel integral
semi-van with sliding cab doors,
pick-up area at rear and drop
tailboard.

1962
Alvis (GB)
'Stalwart' C

Based on the famous FV 600 Alvis range the 'Stalwart' C was the commercial version of the 'Stalwart' FV 622, a 5-ton military cross-country and amphibious load-carrier. First shown at the 1962 International Commercial Motor Show, this six-wheel drive machine was intended primarily for use on oilfield exploration, land reclamation, etc., featuring four-wheel steering at the front, equi-spaced wheels, a 40 mph maximum land speed and 5 knots in water. Only the prototype was constructed.
Engine: Rolls-Royce B.81 Mk 80B 8-cyl. in-line, petrol, 220 bhp.
Transmission: 5-speed with forward and reverse transfer.
Chassis: Integral construction with no chassis frame. Independent suspension. Drive transmitted via six bevel boxes and hub reduction gears to all six wheels. Water propulsion by two Dowty hydrojet units at the rear mechanically driven from the pto.
Bodywork: Alvis standard integral all-steel design with single watertight dropsides.

1962
Studebaker (USA)
Diesel Tractive Unit

This was one of the last commercial types produced under the Studebaker name by the Studebaker-Packard Corporation of South Bend, Indiana. Powered by a Series 53 GM Detroit Diesel announced some four years earlier, it featured cab and bonnet assemblies very similar to those on the smaller 'Transtar' range and was offered in a variety of wheelbase lengths for gross combination weights of between 29,000 and 41,000 lb.
Engine: GM Detroit Diesel Series 53 4-cyl. in-line, diesel, 130 bhp.
Transmission: 4-speed (5-speed or overdrive synchromesh unit optional).
Chassis: Pressed-steel channel-section sidemembers. Semi-elliptic leaf springs all round. Double-reduction rear axle. 9.00×20 tyres all round, duals at rear.
Bodywork: 5th wheel coupling.

1962
ZIL (USSR)
130

For many years the Soviet motor industry was some way behind that of the Western World. Since about 1960, however, considerable strides have been made, notably in the medium-weight commercial and passenger vehicle fields where Western, and particularly American, influences can be seen in most designs. The ZIL '130' was typical of these. Announced in 1961, it was offered as a normal-control 2-axle truck or 8/10-tons capacity tractor unit.
Engine: ZIL V-8, petrol, 135 bhp.
Transmission: 5-speed constant-mesh.
Chassis: Pressed-steel channel-section sidemembers. Semi-elliptic leaf springs all round. Spiral-bevel rear axle. Dual tyres at rear.
Bodywork: Wooden double-dropside cargo body.

1963
AEC (GB)
'Mogul'

The 'Mogul' normal-control 2-axle model was first shown at the 1962 Earls Court Show. It was designed for export. 250 chassis were ordered for South America very early on. The normal-control layout provided maximum engine access and the double-skin insulated cab gave protection against extreme temperatures. A 3-axled version, the 'Majestic', was also available.
Engine: AEC AV691 6-cyl. in-line, diesel, 205 bhp.
Transmission: 6-speed constant-mesh (with overdrive).
Chassis: Pressed-steel channel-section sidemembers with bolted pressed-steel channel-section crossmembers. Semi-elliptic leaf springs with telescopic double-acting hydraulic shock absorbers at front and 'helper' springs at rear. Double-reduction spiral-bevel/double-helical rear axle. B.7×5 steel disc wheels with 11.00×20 tyres, duals at rear.

1963
Hotchkiss (F)
DH 50 N

The 'DH 50 N', a normal-control diesel-powered 5½-tonner, was introduced in 1958, just one year after the petrol version, the 'PL 50 N', had been announced. Production eventually ceased in 1964 when the Company closed certain sections of its manufacturing facilities. During the production period, both the petrol- and diesel-engined models were available as normal- or long-wheelbase types and sold as chassis, chassis/scuttle, chassis/cab or with standard bodywork as shown.

Engine: Hotchkiss 4-cyl. in-line, diesel, 62 bhp.
Transmission: 4-speed.
Chassis: Pressed-steel channel-section sidemembers.
Semi-elliptic leaf springs all round with shock absorbers at front.
6.50 × 20 tyres all round, duals at rear.
Bodywork: Hotchkiss wooden fixed-side body with full canvas tilt.

1963
Lancia (I)
'Superjolly'

One of the lighter models produced by Lancia in more recent years has been the 1½-ton 'Superjolly'. This is offered as a van, pick-up, and other variations, such as ambulance, bus and personnel-carrier. All are built to the same basic specification, a special feature being their low-loading qualities. All versions are available as standard. There are two special designs, one a mobile shop and display unit and the other a motorized living van.

Engine: Model 315.000 4-cyl. horizontally-opposed, petrol, 58 bhp.
Transmission: 3-speed.
Chassis: Independent front suspension. Front-wheel drive.
6.00 × 16 tyres at front, 6.40 × 16 tyres at rear.
Bodywork: Lancia light-alloy pick-up with drop tailgate.

1963
OMT (I)
MF4 8-wheeler

To overcome legislation restricting 6-wheeled rigid models to 18 tons GVW, many Italian manufacturers offered special 8-wheeled conversions for use at 22 tons GVW. Officine Meccaniche Tortonesi Srl. of Tortona designed and built a complete 8-wheeled truck, employing an AEC power unit; and with only one non-steering axle — the foremost axle of the rear bogie. Actual production has reached a three-figure mark.
Engine: AEC AV690 6-cyl. in-line, diesel, 200 bhp.
Transmission: 4-speed with 2-speed auxiliary.
Chassis: Pressed-steel channel-section sidemembers. Pirelli-Saga air suspension at rear axle. Propeller shaft drive to leading axle of rear bogie. Single tyres except on the driven axle.
Bodywork: All-steel double-dropside.

1963
Steyr (A)
586

The products of Steyr-Daimler-Puch AG fall largely into two categories — light off-highway models and medium- and heavy-duty on-highway trucks. The '586' on-highway machine was one of the last normal-control Steyr trucks built. Its front end styling evolved from the 1941 Steyr '1500A' military models. Similar styling was used for the Hungarian Csepe trucks.
Engine: Steyr WD.609b 6-cyl. in-line, diesel, 132 bhp.
Transmission: 5-speed.
Chassis: Welded construction side- and crossmembers of special steel plate. Semi-elliptic leaf springs with telescopic shock absorbers at front. Dual-ratio rear axle with differential lock. 7.00×20 wheels. 9.00×20 (14-ply) tyres, duals at rear.
Bodywork: Steyr all-steel double-dropside tipping body.

1964
Albion (GB)
'Claymore' CL.3AL

In 1958 Albion Motors Ltd. announced two commercial ranges: the
'Chieftain' 7-tonner and 'Claymore'
4/5-tonner. The 'Claymore' series,
with five basic models, became the
most popular light British commercial
featuring an underfloor engine. They
were well known for the 3-man cab
mounted ahead of the front axle.
Shown is a later long-wheelbase
(154 in) model featuring an extra
kerbside observation window in the
door.
Engine: Albion EN.250 4-cyl.
in-line, diesel, 72 bhp.
Transmission: 5-speed.
Chassis: Pressed-steel channel-
section sidemembers. Semi-elliptic
leaf springs. 'I'-section front axle.
Fully-floating spiral-bevel rear axle.
7.50×20 (10-ply) tyres, duals at
rear.
Bodywork: Double-dropside
light-alloy body specially designed by
Bonallack & Sons Ltd. for carrying
scaffold poles. Double-panelled
dropsides and tailboard interchange-
able with existing Bonallack
dropsiders.

118

1964
ALM (F)
TPK4-65P

Specialists in custom-building commercial trucks, Ateliers Legueu Meaux
also offer some on- and off-highway
types, notably of 4×4 and 6×6 configuration. Normal-control models,
such as the 'TPK4-65P' (in tractor
form as the 'TPK4-65MT'), have the
same basic cab, incorporating reinforced fibreglass construction
throughout. British Ford 6-cyl. petrol
and diesel power units available for
several models.
Engine: Perkins 6.305 6-cyl. in-line,
diesel, 143 bhp.
Transmission: 5-speed with
2-speed transfer.
Chassis: Pressed-steel channel-
section sidemembers reinforced
where necessary. Semi-elliptic leaf
springs. ALM Type F60 front axle and
D60 rear axle, both driven. 11.00×20
tyres, duals at rear.
Bodywork: All-steel fixed-side
tipper with protective headboard.
Front-mounted power winch.

1964
Foden (GB)
'Twin-Load' 8AE7/32

Alterations to the British Construction & Use Regulations produced one novel attempt to retain the 8-wheeled rigid vehicle. The revised Regulations favoured articulated machines at 32-tons GCW. The Foden 'Twin-Load' was an 'artic' but consisted of an 8-wheeled 'rigid' with 5th wheel coupling at the rear and a short single-axle semi-trailer behind. This semi-trailer was designed by Fodens, utilizing one of their trailing axles, but assembled by R. A. Dyson & Co. Ltd. Only a handful were built, most going to Messrs Harveys of Bristol.

Engine: Foden FD.6 Mk 7 6-cyl. in-line, diesel, 225 bhp.

Transmission: 4-speed with 3-speed auxiliary.

Chassis: Pressed-steel channel-section sidemembers. Semi-elliptic leaf springs at front. Two semi-elliptic leaf springs at rear bogie. 9.00×20 tyres, duals at rear bogie and semi-trailer.

Bodywork: Two Foden platform bodies.

1964
Volvo (S)
L.4751

This left-hand drive 'L.4751' 7.7 tons capacity model was the first vehicle of this marque to enter service with a British operator. It was loaned by its Swedish makers to Cubitt Town Transport Ltd., who built and fitted the flat body, for assessment trials. The trials proved favourable and Volvo trucks, mainly heavy articulated, are now a common sight on British roads. The UK concessionaire is Ailsa Trucks Ltd., of Glasgow.

Engine: Volvo 6-cyl. in-line, turbocharged diesel, 95 bhp.
Transmission: 5-speed.
Chassis: Pressed-steel 'U'-section sidemembers with riveted crossmembers. Semi-elliptic leaf springs all round, with double-acting hydraulic shock absorbers at front and 'helper' springs at rear. Eaton 2-speed rear axle. 6.5×20 steel disc wheels with 9.00×20 tyres all round, duals at rear.
Bodywork: Wooden flat built by Cubitt Town Transport Ltd.

1965
Bedford (GB)
'R'-Series 4×4

Vauxhall Motors Ltd. is the only British manufacturer to offer a range of four-wheel drive truck chassis for civilian operators as standard, using components common to other heavy models in their range. The 'R'-Series, available in 132- or 158-in. wheelbase, has been superseded by the new 'M'-Series 4×4 but many are still in service.

Engine: Bedford 6-cyl. in-line, petrol, 133 bhp.
Transmission: 4-speed synchromesh with 2-speed transfer.
Chassis: Pressed-steel channel-section sidemembers with riveted and bolted crossmembers. Semi-elliptic leaf springs. Fully-floating hypoid rear axles. 8.25×20 tyres, duals at rear.
Bodywork: Reynolds Boughton all-steel fixed-side tipper with twin front rams, double-skin insulated cab roof and radiator brush guard.

1965
Citroën (F)
T.55 'Sahara'

The 'T.55' four-wheel drive model was specially developed for cross-country use, and in particular for work in tropical or desert areas. It was, strictly, a goods model but a few were supplied with passenger bodywork as shown. The same basic cab design as that employed on many single-axle drive Citroën models was employed. Note high position of engine air intake with extra air cleaner (for use in the Sahara) and kerb observation window in door.

Engine: Citroën 6-cyl. in-line, diesel, 100 bhp.
Transmission: 5-speed with 2-speed transfer.
Chassis: Pressed-steel channel-section. Semi-elliptic leaf springs all round. 11.00×20 tyres all round, duals at rear.
Bodywork: All-steel desert bus.

1965
Unic (F)
'Saverne' MZ 36 HWT

The 'Saverne' was available as a forward-control truck or tractor chassis, a forward-control tractor chassis with automatic coupling, or as a four-wheel drive normal-control machine, type 'MZ 36 HWT'. The latter is illustrated. This featured fuel injection and was suited in particular to on/off-highway tipper applications. The front axle drive conversion was by Herwaythorn, a firm which modified many conventional chassis of various French makes to the all-wheel drive configuration.
Engine: Unic 'Carre' 4-cyl. in-line, diesel, 115 bhp.
Transmission: 4-speed with 2-speed transfer.
Chassis: Pressed-steel channel-section sidemembers with crossmembers of bolted and riveted construction. Semi-elliptic leaf springs all round with 'helper' springs at rear. 9.00 × 20 tyres all round, duals at rear.

1966
Dodge (GB)
KL600 Low-loader

The 23,520 lb GVW Dodge 'KL600'
low-loader was purpose-built for the
distributive trades and municipal
applications, having a 'top of frame'
height when unladen of only 25 in.
It was offered as a 156- or 180-in
wheelbase chassis, powered by a
Perkins 6.354 diesel engine, and
featured the standard Dodge tiltcab.
Engine: Perkins 6.354 6-cyl. in-line,
diesel, 120 bhp.
Transmission: 5-speed
constant-mesh.
Chassis: Pressed-steel channel-
section sidemembers with bolted
channel-section crossmembers.
Semi-elliptic leaf springs all round
with hydraulic telescopic shock
absorbers at front. Single-speed
spiral-bevel rear axle. B6.0×17HD
3-piece 8-stud fixing wheels with
8.25×17 (14-ply) tyres all round,
duals at rear.
Bodywork: Light-alloy flat body.

1966
International (USA)
1700 CO 'Loadstar'

At its first London Commercial Motor Show appearance since before World War II, the International Harvester Co. of Great Britain Ltd. exhibited this forward-control model for the UK market, the '1700 CO Loadstar'. This was only a prototype, specially imported, as production was not due to begin until the following year. As it happened, production never commenced.
Engine: 6-cyl. in-line, diesel, 131 bhp.
Transmission: 5-speed synchromesh.
Chassis: Pressed-steel channel-section sidemembers. Semi-elliptic leaf springs with hydraulic shock absorbers at front. Single-reduction rear axle. B6.5×20 3-piece wheels with 9.00×20 (12-ply) tyres, duals at rear.
Bodywork: 3-way single-dropside composite tipping body.

1966
Leyland (GB)
'Steer'

For 32 tons GCW, Leyland introduced the 'Steer', a tractor with close-coupled first and second steering axle and a driven rear axle. This was necessary to obtain the lightest possible tractor unit to operate at this weight as a combined 5-axle artic. Only three of these units have been built. This one is most unusual as it has a tri-axle semi-trailer.
Engine: Leyland 0.680 6-cyl. in-line, diesel, 153 bhp.
Transmission: 5-speed semi-automatic.
Chassis: Pressed-steel channel-section sidemembers. Semi-elliptic leaf springs. 2-speed rear axle with spiral-bevel epicyclic gear trains. B6.5×20 wheels at front, B7.00×20 at rear. 9.00×20 tyres at front. 10.00×20 duals at rear.
Bodywork: 5th wheel coupling with tri-axle bulk powder tipping tanker semi-trailer.

1966
OeAF (A)
'Hurricane' L7-130

The OeAF (or ÖAF) commercial vehicle range is a direct descendant of the old Austro-Fiat marque. The 'Hurricane', now discontinued, was a smart semi-forward-control type for operation at 13,000 kg GVW. A particularly interesting point was the engine access. The entire bonnet area ahead of the cab was hinged at the forward end providing superb access from either side.

Engine: OeAF 6-cyl. in-line, diesel, 130 bhp.

Transmission: AK 6-55 6-speed.

Chassis: Pressed-steel channel-section sidemembers with riveted crossmembers. Semi-elliptic leaf springs all round with shock absorbers at front and 'helper' springs at rear. Spiral-bevel rear axle. 7.00×20 steel disc wheels with 9.00×20 (14-ply) tyres all round, duals at rear.

Bodywork: Wooden single-dropside cargo body.

1966
Škoda (ČS)
706 RT

The '706 RT' 2-axle truck has now
been in production for a good many
years, with only minor design changes.
The '706'-Series is offered in a number of variations with the '706 RT'
designed specially for long-distance
haulage, often in conjunction with a
drawbar trailer. Crew-cabs and tractor
unit versions are also offered. Although of Škoda design, these trucks
were actually manufactured by the
LIAZ works near Liberec.
Engine: Škoda 706 RT 6-cyl.
in-line, diesel, 160 bhp.
Transmission: 5-speed.
Chassis: Pressed-steel channel-
section sidemembers, with
strengthened rear crossmember.
Semi-elliptic leaf springs with
hydraulic shock absorbers at front.
Driven rear axle with split casing.
8.00×20 wheels with 11.00×20
(16-ply) tyres, duals at rear.
Bodywork: Wooden
single-dropside.

1967
Albion (GB)
'Super Reiver 20' RE.33T

First shown at the 1966 Earls Court Show, the 'Super Reiver 20' was an up-rated version of the 'Super Reiver 19', a 19-tons gross 3-axle chassis announced in 1965. Featuring the Ergomatic tilt-cab, the '20' was offered in two single- and three tandem-drive variations — four for haulage work and the fifth for tipper applications. Three wheelbase lengths were available. Shown is the 'RE.33T' standard tipping model.

Engine: Leyland 'Power-Plus' 0.400 6-cyl. in-line, diesel, 125 bhp.
Transmission: 5-speed constant-mesh (overdrive optional).
Chassis: Pressed-steel channel-section sidemembers with bolted crossmembers. Semi-elliptic leaf springs. 'I'-section front axle. Tandem-drive spiral-bevel rear bogie. Steel disc wheels with 10.00 × 20 (16-ply) tyres, duals at rear.
Bodywork: Light-alloy fixed-side tipper by Gilbraiths Commercials Ltd.

1967
Bedford (GB)
VAS

The 'VAS' is a short-wheelbase bus and coach chassis frequently used for mobile shop work, exhibition units, etc. Petrol or diesel engines are offered, both Bedford units, and wide- or close-ratio transmissions, or a 5-speed overdrive box, are also available. As shown, the 'VAS' operates at 5,105 lb GVW.
Engine: Bedford 6-cyl. in-line, diesel, 100 bhp.
Transmission: 4-speed synchromesh.
Chassis: Pressed-steel channel-section sidemembers with riveted and bolted crossmembers. Semi-elliptic leaf springs and double-acting hydraulic telescopic shock absorbers. Fully-floating spiral-bevel rear axle. 6.00G×16 6-stud-fixing 2-piece wheels with 7.50×16 radial tyres, duals at rear.
Bodywork: Integral mobile library body.

1967
ERF (GB)
64P

Designed and built for operation at 16 tons GVW in the United Kingdom, the '64P' is one of the smallest vehicles in the extensive ERF range. Featuring the now familiar 'LV' cab with 'set forward' entry, the 64P is ideally suited for operation as a 'rigid' vehicle. Gardner, Cummins and Rolls-Royce engines are also available, model designations being '64G', '64Cu' and '64R' respectively.
Engine: Perkins 6.354 6-cyl. in-line, diesel, 120 bhp.
Transmission: ENV 542 SMA 5-speed.
Chassis: Pressed-steel channel-section sidemembers. Semi-elliptic leaf springs all round. 10.00×20 (16-ply) tyres at front. 18.00×22.5 (18-ply) 'Super Singles' at rear.
Bodywork: Concrete-mixing equipment.

129

1967
ZUK (PL)
A-13 Pick-up

The ZUK 'A-13 Pick-up' is the basic type of ZUK light commercial produced by the FSC-Lublin plant. This compact design, which is also available as an integral van, dropside truck, fire appliance, ambulance, etc., is designed to carry a 900 kg payload plus two crew members. Two engines are offered — the 'ZUK S-21' 77 bhp petrol unit or the Perkins 4.108 diesel.

Engine: Perkins 4.108 4-cyl. in-line, diesel, 52 bhp.

Transmission: 3-speed (with synchromesh on 2nd and 3rd).

Chassis: Steel rectangular tube sidemembers. Independent coil spring suspension at front. Semi-elliptic leaf springs at rear. Single-reduction bevel-gear final drive at rear axle. 6.50×16 tyres all round.

Bodywork: ZUK all-steel fixed-side integral pick-up with drop tailboard and full-tilt cover.

1968
Atkinson (GB)
'Silver Knight, BT.10066C

One of the largest and most powerful vehicles exhibited at the 1968 Earls Court Motor Show, was a custom-built tractor for Pickfords Heavy Haulage Ltd., designed for a gross combination weight of 224,000 lb. Being a normal-control model, this was rather unusual for Atkinson Vehicles Ltd. although some items normally applied to their standard truck range were incorporated in the design.
Engine: Cummins NH250 6-cyl. in-line, diesel, 250 bhp.
Transmission: Allison CLBT 4460 'Torqmatic' 6-speed semi-automatic.
Chassis: Pressed-steel channel-section sidemembers. Two semi-elliptic leaf springs at rear bogie. Kirkstall hypoid-bevel tandem-drive rear bogie. Michelin 'Sahara' 12.00×20 tyres, duals at rear.
Bodywork: Later fitted with ballast box and power winch for use as drawbar heavy haulage tractor.

131

1968
Bedford (GB)
KME

This first standard 'KM'-Series 6-wheeled truck, was probably the first Bedford 6-wheeler assembled entirely on the Company's own production line. Based on a long-wheelbase 'KM'-Series chassis, it was announced in 1968, being available as a 20- or 22-tons GVW machine, depending upon wheelbase length.

Engine: Bedford 6-cyl. in-line, diesel, 143 bhp.
Transmission: 5-speed.
Chassis: Pressed-steel channel-section sidemembers. Semi-elliptic leaf springs all round with telescopic dampers, and balance-beam linkage system at rear bogie. B7.5 wheels all round with 10.00×20 radial tyres, duals at rear.
Bodywork: Triple-dropside wooden body.

1968
Unipower (GB)
'Invader'

Replacing the 'Hannibal' and 'Forester' four-wheel drive models, the Unipower 'Invader' is designed as a rigid at up to 16 tons GVW, according to wheelbase, and as a tractor for up to 26 tons GCW, as a drawbar or fifth wheel outfit. The Motor Panels forward-control cab was on the prototype chassis shown, although future 'production' models may carry Unipower's own cab.
Engine: Perkins V8.510 V-8, diesel, 170 bhp.
Transmission: 5-speed synchromesh with 2-speed transfer.
Chassis: Pressed-steel channel-section sidemembers with bolted crossmembers. Semi-elliptic leaf springs.
Double-reduction axles at front and rear. 3-piece steel disc wheels with 10.00×20 (16-ply) tyres.
Bodywork: Temporary ballast box.

1969
Hino   (J)
KM400

The Japanese motor industry is rapidly
expanding. Hino entered the European
market some years ago through a
Dutch assembly plant and a similar
set-up based in Dublin. The 'KM400'
is typical of Hino models offered in
Ireland, being designed for a GVW of
19,140 lb. Hino's origins date back to
1917 when it was formed by the
Tokyo Gas & Electric Co. During the
1960s Hino introduced a wide range
of medium- and heavy-duty trucks,
also buses.
Engine: Hino DM100 6-cyl.
in-line, diesel, 90 bhp.
Transmission: 4-speed (5-speed
optional).
Chassis: Pressed-steel channel-
section sidemembers. Semi-elliptic
leaf springs with 'helper' springs at
rear axle and shock absorbers at front.
7.50×16 tyres, duals at rear.
Bodywork: Hino wooden
single-dropside.

1969
Oshkosh (USA)
R-2034-IE-I

The Oshkosh Truck Corporation prides itself on being able to build any vehicle to the customer's own requirements. In 1969 there were eight basic models, from snowploughs and truck-mixers to multi-axle specials and forward- and normal-control road tractors. This machine is one of the more normal tandem-drive long-distance trunking tractors. In addition, the Oshkosh Truck Corporation offers a special re-manufacturing service whereby earlier models are brought in and completely rebuilt to the latest design for two-thirds the price of a new vehicle.

Engine: 6-cyl. in-line, diesel, 250 bhp.

Transmission: 16-speed with 2-speed auxiliary.

Chassis: Pressed-steel channel-section sidemembers. Semi-elliptic leaf springs all round. 10.00×20 tyres all round, duals at rear.

Bodywork: 5th wheel coupling.

1970
Diamond Reo (USA)
CO-7864D

Diamond Reo Trucks, a Division of White Motor Corporation, was formed in 1967 by the amalgamation of the Diamond T and Reo Motor Truck Divisions of the Corporation. Now specializing in the design and manufacture of construction equipment vehicles (i.e. truck-mixers, tippers, etc.), the Company also produces lighter 2-axle on-highway models and heavier forward- and normal-control on-highway motive units, notably of 6-wheeled layout.

Engine: Cummins NH-220 6-cyl. in-line, diesel, 212 bhp.
Transmission: Spicer 7453A 5-speed.
Chassis: Heat-treated steel sidemembers with crossmembers of bolted lock-nut construction. Rubber tandem suspension at rear. Rockwell FF-901 front axle. Rockwell tandem-drive rear bogie. Dual tyres at rear.
Bodywork: 5th wheel coupling with light-alloy stepframe tandem-axle livestock semi-trailer.

1970
OM (I)
'Daino' 40

Although the OM concern is now part of the giant Fiat organization, it continues to produce an extensive range of trucks and passenger vehicles to its own design. Representative of the lighter goods models is the 'Daino', available as the 'Daino' 40 or 45, for 4,000 and 4,500 kg payload respectively. These machines can be supplied with or without the standard factory-built body shown here.
Engine: OM CO3/21 4-cyl. in-line, diesel, 87 bhp.
Transmission: 5-speed (synchromesh on 3rd, 4th and 5th).
Chassis: Pressed-steel channel-section sidemembers. Semi-elliptic leaf springs all round. Fully-floating overhead-worm rear axle. 7.50 × 16 (14-ply) tyres, duals at rear.
Bodywork: OM all-steel single-dropside body.

1970
Scania (S)
LBS 110

Recently Scania trucks have become a leading marque for long-distance haulage and for TIR work. The 'LBS 110' is offered as a 6-wheeled rigid or artic and the former is popular for operation with drawbar trailer. A more powerful 6-wheeler known as the 'LBT' range, was announced recently.
Engine: Scania D11R06 6-cyl. in-line, diesel, 202 bhp.
Transmission: Scania G601 5-speed synchromesh.
Chassis: 'U'-Section steel sidemembers with riveted crossmembers. Semi-elliptic leaf springs with double-acting shock absorbers at front. Single-drive rear bogie. 8.00×20 steel disc wheels with 11.00×20 (16-ply) tyres, duals at rear.
Bodywork: 5th wheel coupling with tandem-axle full-tilt TIR semi-trailer.

1970
Star (PL)
660D 6×6

Polish Star commercial vehicles have been produced since 1949. This six-wheel drive forward-control model was designed for military use and some have been exported to Africa. For on-highway use the GVW is 4,400 kg but off-road this is limited to 3,500 kg. It is offered as a chassis-cab, tilt truck (as shown) or with full breakdown and workshop equipment. A petrol-engined version, the '660M2', is available.
Engine: Star S530A1 6-cyl. in-line, diesel, 100 bhp.
Transmission: 5-speed with 2-speed transfer.
Chassis: Welded steel frame. Semi-elliptic leaf springs with hydraulic shock absorbers at front. Single-reduction bevel-gear final drive. 12.00×18 single tyres.
Bodywork: Star soft-top cab and composite sided body with full canvas tilt.

1971
Berna (CH)
5V

Although the Swiss Saurer and Berna marques remain separate
so far as name and model designations are concerned, the
vehicles themselves are identical. The Berna '5V', for instance,
is identical to the Saurer '5D', both being designed and
constructed as tandem-drive 6-wheeled tippers, particularly
suited for off-highway work. A 4-wheeled version is also
offered.
Engine: D1KL 6-cyl. in-line, diesel, 275 bhp.
Transmission: 4-speed.
Chassis: Pressed-steel channel-section sidemembers of
heavy-duty construction. 12.00×20 tyres all round, duals at
rear.
Bodywork: 3-way single-dropside light-alloy tipper with
single underbody hydraulic ram.

1971
Berna (CH)
S2VF

Berna's 'S2VF' forward-control model, for 14,200 kg GVW, is
similarly identical to the Saurer 'S2DF'. This model is offered in
two wheelbase lengths – 3,800 mm and 4,500 mm – both
powered by a 160 bhp diesel engine. Motorwagenfabrik Berna
AG are now a wholly-owned subsidiary of AG Adolph Saurer.
Thus, most components are standardized. The 'S2VF' can also
be used with a drawbar trailer for operation at 26,000 kg GCW.
Engine: T5 6-cyl. in-line, diesel, 160 bhp.
Transmission: 5-speed.
Chassis: 'U'-section steel sidemembers. Semi-elliptic leaf
springs all round with telescopic shock absorbers at front.
7.50×20 wheels with 10.00×20 tyres all round, duals at rear.
Bodywork: Double-dropside side-loading pallet truck.

1971
De Soto   (TR)
PD-600

Although De Soto trucks are, generally, no longer in production, the
Turkish Chrysler plant still produces a
variety of models under this name,
utilizing a cab and front end specially
designed by Chrysler (USA) for local
manufacture in developing countries.
One of these is the normal-control
'PF-600' for 10,764 kg GVW. Most
of the other vehicles in this series are
for lighter applications, the majority
being of the pick-up variety. Chrysler
Sanayi supplies these models under
the Dodge and Fargo names also.
Engine: Perkins 6.354 6-cyl. in-line,
diesel, 130 bhp.
Transmission: 5-speed.
Chassis: Pressed-steel channel-
section sidemembers. Semi-elliptic
leaf springs all round. Fully-floating
rear axle. 9.00 × 20 tyres all round,
duals at rear.

1971
Seddon-Deutz (GB)
'13-Four'

The fruit of recent co-operation between Magirus-Deutz (Great Britain) Ltd. and Seddon Motors Ltd. is a unique Deutz-engined Seddon '13-Four', which makes regular runs from Britain to the German Ulm works (carrying British tyres for chassis for the U.K., returning with spares to back up the Magirus-Deutz service network).

Engine: Deutz F6L 912 V-6, diesel, 120 bhp.

Transmission: 2F AK5-35 5-speed constant-mesh.

Chassis: Pressed-steel channel-section sidemembers. Semi-elliptic leaf springs with telescopic shock absorbers at front. 'I'-section front axle. Eaton 18802 2-speed rear axle. B7.5 steel disc wheels and 10.00 × 20 (16-ply) tyres, duals at rear.

Bodywork: All-steel double-dropside with full canvas tilt for TIR work.

1971
Terberg (NL)
N800

The 'N800' six-wheel drive truck features ex-US Army 'M'-Series axles and a DAF engine. Automobielbedrijf en Machinefabriek W.G. Terberg & Zn, Benschop NV, specializes in the design of tandem- and six-wheel drive 3-axle trucks assembled from proprietary units on modified ex-military chassis.
Engine: DAF DD575 6-cyl. in-line, diesel, 120 bhp.
Transmission: ZF AK 5-35-2 5-speed.
Chassis: Reinforced pressed-steel channel-section sidemembers. Semi-elliptic leaf springs all round. Fully-floating top-mounted double-reduction final drive axles. 9.00×20 (12-ply) tyres, duals at rear.
Bodywork: Special liquid concrete pumping equipment. Front-mounted power winch.

1972
Bedford (GB)
'KH'-Series

The 'KH'-Series (one of the lines in the 'TK' range) Bedford 14½-tonner has been completely revised for 1972. Specification changes include a heavier duty front axle for better load distribution, an increased payload capacity, improved braking systems, and still greater driver comfort. Externally, the new version looks much the same as other 'TK' models, apart from the 'KM'-style wide front wings, slightly higher cab mounting, and front flashing indicators to either side of the headlamps.
Engine: Bedford 466 6-cyl. in-line, diesel, 143 bhp.
Transmission: 5-speed synchromesh.
Chassis: Pressed-steel channel-section sidemembers. Semi-elliptic leaf springs with shock absorbers all round. 10.00×20 tyres all round, duals at rear.
Bodywork: Bedford wooden double-dropside body.

1972
Unic (F)
T 340 A

Following the amalgamation of design and manufacturing interests between the French Unic concern and Fiat of Italy in 1970, a number of new models were introduced. Early in 1971 the Unic 'T 340 A' 35/38-ton GCW heavy tractor unit was announced. This incorporates a considerable quantity of Fiat components, most noticeable being the cab. A brand new and extremely powerful V-8 engine was introduced for this model.

Engine: Unic V 85 S V-8, diesel, 340 bhp.

Transmission: Unic B190 8-speed synchromesh.

Chassis: Pressed-steel channel-section sidemembers. Semi-elliptic leaf springs all round with telescopic shock absorbers at front and 'helper' springs at rear. 12.00×20 V10 wheels with F.20 XT tyres all round, duals at rear.

Bodywork: 5th wheel coupling with tandem-axle 'skeletal' container semi-trailer.

Index